HUMAN PSYCHOLOGY FOR BUSINESS

An introduction to Personality, Thinking, Behaviour, Motivation, Intelligence, and Decision-Making

Dr. Dennis Wilson, PhD, MBA

◆ FriesenPress

Suite 300 - 990 Fort St
Victoria, BC, V8V 3K2
Canada

www.friesenpress.com

Copyright © 2019 by Dr. Dennis Wilson
First Edition — 2019

Dr. Dennis Wilson
3021 Winger Road, RR2
Stevensville, Ontario, Canada, L0S 1S0
647-272-9866
dr.wilson@wilson-research.ca

All rights reserved.

No part of this publication may be reproduced in any form, or by any means, electronic or mechanical, including photocopying, recording, or any information browsing, storage, or retrieval system, without permission in writing from FriesenPress.

ISBN
978-1-5255-2757-9 (Hardcover)
978-1-5255-2758-6 (Paperback)
978-1-5255-2759-3 (eBook)

1. BUSINESS & ECONOMICS, HUMAN RESOURCES & PERSONNEL MANAGEMENT

Distributed to the trade by The Ingram Book Company

Table of Contents

Purpose of this Book 1

Introduction 3

Brain Physiology 7
    Neurons 7
    The Energy Engine 14

Brain Structure and Function 31

The Unique Brain 39
    Feelings and Emotions 41
    Emotions and Motivation.. 44

Decision-Making 47
    Why Decisions Go Wrong . 50
    Controlling for Flawed Decisions 54

Talents and Aptitudes 59

Male and Female Differences . 61

Introverts and Extroverts 63

Implications to Management . 65

Psychometrics 67
    Validity and Reliability 67
    Psychological Profiling 68
    Models and Categorization . 69

The Psychometric Proposition 71

Concepts In Psychology That Are Relevant To Business 73
    Intelligence 73
    Aptitude 74
    Skills.................. 76

Emotional Intelligence 79
    Ability Model 80
    Trait Model............. 81
    Mixed Model 81

Personality Theories 85
  16-Personality-Factor Theory 86
  Big Five Personality Trait
  Theory 87
  Enneagram 89
  True Colors 93
  Myers-Briggs Type Indicator 94
  Personality 96

Thinking 99
  Herrmann Brain Dominance
  Instrument 99
  Personality and Thinking . 101

Behaviour 103
  DISC 104
  Thinking and Behaviour . . 106

Talents 111

**Combining Assessment
Instruments** 115

**Practical Application of
Psychometric Assessments** . . 117

**Other Popular Psychometric
Products Specific To Business** 119
  Kolbe 119
  Emergenetics 120
  Winslow 122
  Taylor Protocols 123
  California Psychological
  Inventory (CPI) 123
  FIRO Business 124

**Psychometric Assessments and the
Workplace** 125

Advancing the Topic 127

In Review 133

The Right Horse for the Job . 135

Index 137

Purpose of this Book

In the field of human psychology, there is a rapidly expanding body of knowledge based on an ever-more-solid base of empirical research. What was basically theory in the 1900s is now being verified and substantiated with such current technology as Brain Wave Research, fMRI (Functional Magnetic Resonance Imaging), and CAT (Computer Axial Tomography) scans. These technologies enable researchers to peer inside the active brain and observe its functioning. A more thorough understanding of the brain and brain function allows us to better understand how the brain works, and from this knowledge, we can have a better understanding and appreciation of how humans function. These advancements and this growing body of knowledge are significant, and this knowledge needs to be promoted to young adults joining the workforce. It also needs to be promoted in the business environment, where it can contribute to higher performance and competitive advantage. In general, a better understanding of human psychology leads to improvements in self-esteem, communication, problem-solving, training, customer service, money-management, sales performance, conflict resolution, team performance, and leadership. It also results in lower frustration, greater trust, and enhanced peace of mind. The introduction of any of these elements to the business environment will improve business performance. There is, however, a shortage of textbooks suitable for teaching introductory human psychology in a way that's specifically designed for a business audience.

Thanks to the digital age and wonders of the internet, much of the information provided in this book is freely available—and in great detail, especially on Wikipedia. In addition, there are sites established by universities and academics that publish an extensive amount of data on neurobiology and psychology. Students and the general public may have access to journals and periodicals, as well. This text pulls together, in an abbreviated format, only a relatively small amount of this expanse of available information.

My objective in writing this book is to alert the reader to the differences in people based on a growing body of research, and to promote a respect for those differences. In addition, I hope to introduce the reader to a small portion of the information available as a basis from which they might pursue a more in-depth study of human psychology on their own initiative, especially from a business perspective.

The amount of information provided in this book should be sufficient to establish in the reader's mind a certain amount of faith in the value and utility that can be gained from even a basic level of awareness and understanding of human psychology, and the text will hopefully provide insight into the benefits that may be derived by business.

Introduction

Every individual operates according to different ways of thinking and behaving that are more enjoyable, more natural, easier to manifest, and require less expended energy for them.

One day, my wife and I were driving on an interstate highway in Texas. We were passing the construction of a new interchange and I started to marvel at what I was seeing. My mind launched into thoughts about the size and complexity of the project. I could imagine the volumes of concrete and steel that would go into the construction and the engineering challenge that would have one section of the overpass lining up exactly with another. I was thinking of the manpower involved in the building of the interchange, and the project management needed to keep the work coordinated and moving forward in an organized fashion. I was thinking about the money needed to finance the project, the taxes needed to raise the money, and even the politics and government bureaucracy needed to develop and initiate the project.

Having been abandoned by me (to my thoughts), my wife eventually said to me, "Are you thinking about something?"

With these thoughts fresh in my mind, I proceeded to share my marvel over the construction project. She listened politely but did not share my excitement. When I finished my tale of wonder, she looked at me and casually said, "You should think more about people."

Obviously, my wife and I do not always share the same interests; in fact, our brains function quite differently, resulting in very different interests and very different talents—we have, in fact, totally different personalities.

Is my wife right? Should I think more about people? Or should my wife have a greater appreciation for the differences in people, and allow me my individuality?

Image 1 should be easily recognizable as a picture of a fingerprint. It has some general characteristics that make it recognizable, while at the same time, it is generally understood that each individual's fingerprints are different—unique to the individual.

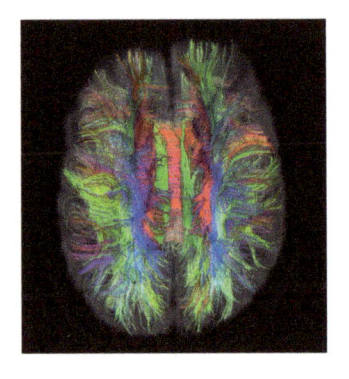

Image 1, fingerprint.

Image 2 is a colour-enhanced MRI of a brain.
(Ruopeng Wang, The Athinoula A. Martinos Center for Biomedical Imaging at Massachusetts General Hospital)

Notice that, like the fingerprint, the brain has a generally recognizable structure and that, also like the fingerprint, each individual's brain is different—unique to the individual. Brains differ in many aspects: the number of neurons, cells, and synapses; the speed with which the neurons transfer a signal; the frequency of a signal; the number and effectiveness of memory cells. There's a vast number of ways in which brains can differ, and each of the differences contributes to some differential performance in mental function that ends up defining us, our talents, interests, and abilities—essentially, who we are.

Neuroscientists are a new breed of researchers, and they are drawn from about twenty different disciplines, including psychology. They are guided by the assumption that everything the brain does is ultimately explainable by biological and chemical events taking place within it. These can be events that unfold throughout the entire brain or that occur exclusively in a particular region of the brain. To these researchers, understanding behaviour means knowing its biological foundation.

This reminds me of a conversation I had with a fellow student many years ago when we were both young and naïve undergraduates. I was expressing my excitement about the possibility of all human functions, including brain function, being explained in terms of biology. My friend responded to the effect that, since biology is basically physics and chemistry, and since physics and chemistry are basically explainable in mathematical terms, it all comes down to mathematics. I marveled at the idea that the world, including people, could be explained in mathematical terms.

However, for now, I will stick with the neuroscientists' viewpoint, and will proceed initially with an understanding of human psychology from a biological perspective. One of the first biological factors to consider with respect to the development of the brain is human genetics. At least a third of the approximately 20,000 different genes that make up the human genome are primarily expressed in the brain. This is the highest proportion of genes expressed in any part of the body. (http://www.ninds.nih.gov/disorders/brain_basics/genes_at_work.htm, 04/14/2015)

Each brain, though genetically designed to have a familiar general structure and the same functional components, is also genetically structured to be unique. There are individually unique brain structures dictated by genetics. There are also the accumulations of individual life experiences that contribute to learning and memory development, to say nothing of how life experiences may impact the brain and alter its physical structure and performance. Among these life experiences, we find both such simple incursions as bumps, bruises, and hypoxia, along with the more complex effects caused by a person's physical environment. Consider, in this category, pathogens, the nutritive aspects of an individual's early-childhood development, and exposure to electrical currents and shocks, chemicals, and radiation.

As expressed above, genetics are expressed in the development of a physiologically unique brain. A simple understanding of basic brain structure and physiology helps to reveal those aspects of the brain that are unique to an individual and which might result in differential brain performance.

Achieving this basic understanding of brain physiology calls for a rudimentary understanding of the nervous system and its core component, the nerve or neuron. Neurons exist in groups that form functional nerve structures within the body and brain. Each functional structure is typically acknowledged to serve some specific function. For example, within the larger brain structure, there is specialization with respect to the left and right hemispheres, visual and audio centres, memory, pain and pleasure, emotions, etc. This is not an exhaustive list of specialized brain function, but it should be sufficient to give the reader an appreciation of the breadth of variability in brain function and performance, and of the scope of variability that can exist across individuals.

Brain Physiology

Neurons

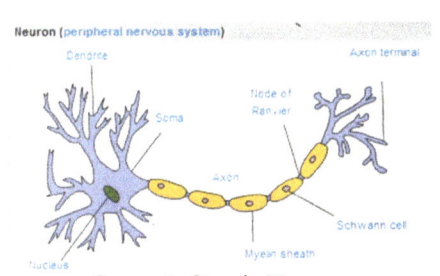

Image 3, Simple Neuron

In very simple terms, a nerve is composed of one or more neurons. Neurons are the core components of the nervous system, which includes the brain, spinal cord, and peripheral ganglia.

According to Wikipedia, the term neuron was coined by the German anatomist Heinrich Wilhelm Waldeyer. The neuron was first recognized as the primary functional unit of the nervous system in the early twentieth century through the work of the Spanish anatomist Santiago Ramón y Cajal. He proposed that neurons were discrete cells that communicated with each other via specialized junctions—or spaces—between cells. The spaces are called synapses.

Life of a Neuron

Previously, it was believed that neurons did not undergo cell division after prenatal and infant development. One Harvard website indicates that, in the first few years of life, 700 new neural connections are formed every second. After this period of rapid proliferation neural connections (infant development), connections are reduced through a process called pruning, so that brain circuits become more efficient (http://developingchild.harvard.edu/resources/inbrief-science-of-ecd/). Beyond this early period of development, the consensus was that the nervous system could not grow new neurons. Recent research, however, has shown that some adult neurogenesis (growth of new neurons) does occur. New neurons, it turns out, can originate from neural stem cells found throughout the brain—good news for individuals who suffer nerve damage. But it should be noted that this regenerative activity in the adult brain is very limited—so limited, in fact, that the theory that neurogenesis ceases in early childhood is still widely accepted.

It is understood that a person's potential brain cell count may be coded in their genes, and that, with the exception of some possible, though very limited, further neurogenesis an individual's number of brain cells is provisioned at an early age. After that, a person's brain cells are subject to only refinement and destruction over the course of their life. Indeed, we can infer that, as we grow older, we function with ever-diminishing brain capacity courtesy of activities and life experiences (air hypoxia, chemicals, alcohol, contusions, etc.) that tend to destroy brain cells. At the same time, it should be understood that, while there is a decreasing number of neurons, there is an increasing number of dendritic and synaptic connections. It is this process of increasing and revising neuronal connections that is thought to result in learning, improved mental performance, and the accumulation of memories.

Neurons are highly specialized for the processing and the transmission of signals at the cellular level. Given the diversity of functions performed by neurons in different parts of the nervous system, it should not be surprising that there is considerable variety in their shape, size, and electrochemical properties.

A typical neuron has three components: the soma or cell body, dendrites, and an axon. Where the dendrites and axon are functionally specific, the soma can be viewed generally as similar to a typical cell body. The axon and dendrites are filaments that extend from the soma. Dendrites are thin structures that arise from the cell body, often extending for hundreds of micrometres and branching multiple times, giving rise to a complex "dendritic tree." An axon is a special cellular extension that extends from the cell body at a site called the axon hillock and travels for a distance that is possibly as far as one metre in humans, and even longer in other species.

To minimize metabolic activity while maintaining rapid conduction, many neurons have sheaths of myelin around their axons. The sheaths are composed of glial cells—oligodendrocytes in the central nervous system and Schwann cells in the peripheral nervous system. The myelin sheath enables action potentials to travel faster than in unmyelinated axons of the same diameter, and it lowers the amount of energy (metabolic activity) required to propagate the signal. The myelin sheath in peripheral nerves normally runs along the axon in sections about one millimetre long, punctuated by unsheathed nodes called the Nodes of Ranvier, which contain a high density of voltage-gated ion channels. As a general rule, all individuals have axons covered with myelinated sheaths, but there are individual differences in the properties of the myelinated sheaths that result in performance differences. Some people have axons that conduct signals faster or function more efficiently than other individuals.

An item of note with respect to the axon: Multiple sclerosis is a neurological disorder that results from the demyelination of axons in the central nervous system. The loss of myelin on the axon slows down or disrupts the transmission of nerve signals.

The cell body of a neuron frequently gives rise to multiple dendrites, but never to more than one axon, although the axon may branch hundreds of times before it terminates. In the typical nerve impulse, signals are sent from the axon of one neuron to a dendrite of another neuron. There are, however, some exceptions to the typical configuration for a nerve cell, including neurons that lack dendrites, neurons that have no axon, synapses that connect one axon to another axon, or a dendrite interacting with another dendrite. It should be kept in mind that there are only a few exceptions—a fortunate thing, from a cognitive perspective.

There are several stimuli that can activate a neuron leading to electrical activity, including pressure, stretch, chemical interaction, and changes in electric potential across the cell membrane. Any of these stimuli can cause specific ion channels within the cell membrane to open, leading to a flow of ions through it, changing the membrane potential.

Some neurons do not generate action potentials, but instead generate a graded electrical signal, which in turn causes a graded neurotransmitter release. Such non-spiking neurons tend to be sensory neurons—or interneurons—because they cannot carry signals long distances.

All neurons are electrically excitable, maintaining voltage gradients across their membranes by means of metabolically (chemical reactions within a cell body) driven ion pumps, which combine with ion channels embedded in the membrane to generate intracellular-versus-extracellular concentration differences of ions such as sodium, potassium, chloride, and calcium. Changes in the cross-membrane voltage can alter the function of voltage-dependent ion channels. If the voltage changes by a large enough amount, an all-or-none electrochemical pulse called an action potential is generated. The action potential travels rapidly along the cell's axon, and activates synaptic connections with other cells.

Connectivity
Synapse

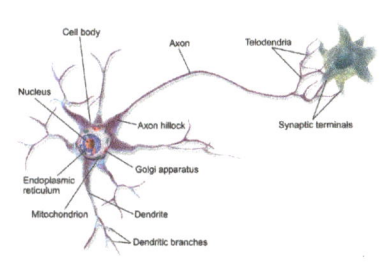

Image 4,
Internal Structure of a Neuron

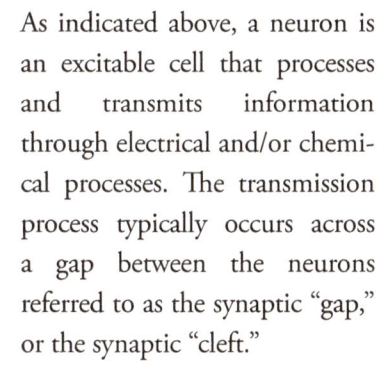

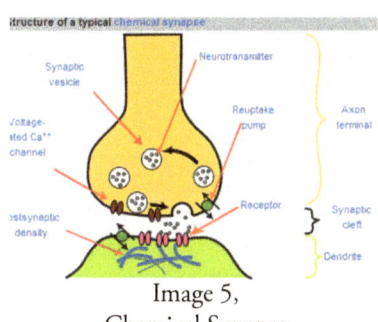

Image 5,
Chemical Synapse

As indicated above, a neuron is an excitable cell that processes and transmits information through electrical and/or chemical processes. The transmission process typically occurs across a gap between the neurons referred to as the synaptic "gap," or the synaptic "cleft."

Neurons communicate across a synapse through a chemical and/or electrical process referred to as synaptic transmission. At a synapse, an axon terminal of one cell comes into very close proximity with, but seldom touches, another neuron's dendrite, soma, or, less commonly, axon. Neurons such as Purkinje cells in the cerebellum can have over 1,000 dendritic branches, making connections with tens of thousands of other cells. Other neurons, such as the magnocellular (visual) neurons of the supraoptic nucleus (a nucleus of magnocellular neurosecretory cells), have only one or two dendrites, each of which receives thousands of synapses.

The fundamental stimulus to a synaptic transmission is the action potential (a propagating electrical signal) that is generated by exploiting the electrically excitable membrane of the neuron. This is also known as a wave of depolarization.

A synapse is viewed as either a chemical synapse or an electrical synapse, with the former far more prominent. Synapses are also classified as either excitatory (increases activity in the target neuron) or inhibitory (decreases activity in the target neuron). The neuron carrying the signal to the synapse is called the presynaptic neuron, and the neuron affected by the interaction at the synapse is called the postsynaptic neuron. Both the presynaptic and postsynaptic sites contain extensive arrays of molecular machinery that link the two membranes together and carry out the signaling process. In many synapses, the presynaptic part is located on an axon, but some presynaptic sites are located on a dendrite or on the soma. In addition, there are cells referred to as astrocytes, which also exchange information with the synaptic neurons, responding to synaptic activity and, in turn, regulating neurotransmission.

Chemical Synapse

A chemical synapse is actually partly electrical and partly chemical. The electrical aspect depends on properties of the neuron's membrane. As with all animal cells, every neuron is surrounded by a plasma membrane—a bilayer of lipid molecules with many types of protein structures embedded in it. Typically, a lipid bilayer is a powerful electrical insulator, but in neurons, many of the protein structures embedded in the membrane are actually electrically active. These include ion channels that permit electrically charged ions to flow across/through the membrane, and ion pumps that actively transport ions from one side of the membrane to the other. Most ion channels are permeable only to specific types of ions, such as sodium (Na^+), potassium (K^+), chloride (Cl^-), and calcium (Ca^{2+}). The interactions between ion channels and ion pumps produce the voltage difference across the membrane—typically a bit less than a tenth of a volt at the baseline. This voltage has two functions: first, it provides a power source for an assortment of voltage-dependent protein machinery embedded in the membrane; second, it provides a basis for electrical signal transmission between different parts of the membrane.

A voltage-gated channel is a channel that is switched between open and closed states by altering the voltage difference across the membrane. Other channels are chemically gated, meaning that they can be switched between open and closed states by interactions with chemicals that diffuse through the extracellular fluid.

> **Electric Eel (http://en.wikipedia.org/wiki/Electric_eel)**
> The electric eel is capable of generating powerful electric shocks of up to 860 volts, which it uses for hunting, self-defense, and communicating with fellow eels. It has three abdominal pairs of organs that are responsible for producing the electricity: the "main organ," the "Hunter's organ," and the "Sach's organ." These organs are made of electrocytes (cells specifically structured to produce an electric charge) lined up so a current of ions can flow through them and stacked so each one adds to an electrical potential difference. In certain situations (hunting, defending, attracting), the eel's brain will send a signal through its nervous system to the electrocytes. This signal opens the ion channels, allowing sodium to flow through, reversing the polarity momentarily. This is a process that is similar to the chemically gated synapses found in nerve cells. The sudden difference in electric potential generates an <u>electric current</u> in a manner similar to a <u>battery</u>, and like the cells of a battery arranged in sequence, the electrocytes of an electric eel are arranged in plates and stacked in series with each plate producing an electric potential difference, which in summation ends up being quite significant.

Electrical Synapse

In an electrical synapse, the presynaptic and postsynaptic cell membranes are connected by special channels called gap junctions that are capable of passing electric current, which causes voltage changes in the presynaptic cell to induce voltage changes in the postsynaptic cell. The main advantage of an electrical synapse is the rapid transfer of signals it inspires from one cell to the next.

THE ENERGY ENGINE

In neurons, as in other cells in the body, the energy engine driving these processes is a substance called Adenosine Triphosphate (ATP). In addition to affecting ion channels, concentrations of calcium in the axon terminal will trigger mitochondrial calcium uptake, which, in turn, activates mitochondrial energy metabolism to produce ATP. Adenosine Triphosphate transports chemical energy within cells for metabolism, and it is used by enzymes and structural proteins in such processes as biosynthetic reactions, motility, and cell division. Remember that brain activity consumes energy. An individual can become mentally as well as physically fatigued, and different individuals will become fatigued at different rates.

Synapses and Memory

Synaptic plasticity is the ability of synapses to strengthen or weaken over time in response to increases or decreases in their activity. Synaptic plasticity may also result from the change in the number of neurotransmitter receptors located on a synapse. There are several underlying mechanisms that cooperate to achieve synaptic plasticity, including changes in the quantity of neurotransmitters released into a synapse and changes in how effectively cells respond to those neurotransmitters. Synaptic plasticity in both excitatory and inhibitory synapses has been found to be dependent upon postsynaptic calcium release. Since memories are postulated to be represented by vastly interconnected networks of synapses in the brain; synaptic plasticity has been found to be one of the important neurochemical foundations of learning and memory (see Hebbian theory). (http://

en.wikipedia.org/wiki/Synaptic_plasticity). As neurotransmitters activate receptors across the synaptic gap, the connection between the two neurons is strengthened when both neurons are active at the same time as a result of the receptor's signaling mechanisms. The strength of two connected neural pathways is thought to result in the storage of information, otherwise known as memory. This process of synaptic strengthening is also known as long-term potentiation.

All-or-None Principle

The conduction of nerve impulses is an example of an all-or-none response. In other words, if a neuron responds at all, then it must respond completely. Greater intensity of stimulation does not produce a stronger signal but can produce a higher frequency of firing. There are differing types of receptor responses to various stimuli. Slowly adapting or tonic receptors respond to steady stimuli and produce a steady rate of firing. These tonic receptors most often respond to increased intensity of stimuli by increasing their firing frequency, usually as a power function of stimuli plotted against impulses per second. This can be likened to an intrinsic property of light where the strength of a photon is not increased or decreased, so in order to get a greater intensity of a specific frequency (colour) of light, there needs to be a greater number of photons.

There is a number of other receptor types, an example of which is the quickly adapting or phasic receptor. In these receptors, the firing decreases or stops with steady stimulation. For example, when skin is touched by an object, the touch causes the neurons to fire, but if the object maintains even pressure against the skin, the neurons stop firing. The Pacinian corpuscle is a skin receptor that functions in this way. It is

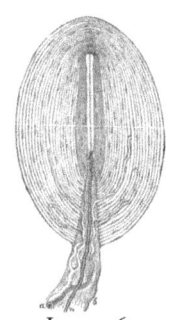

Image 6, Pacinian Corpuscle

structured with concentric layers like an onion, which form around the axon terminal. When pressure is applied and the corpuscle is deformed, the mechanical stimulus is transferred to the axon, which fires. If the pressure is steady, the axon ceases to fire; thus, these neurons respond with a transient depolarization during the initial deformation, and again when the pressure is removed, causing the corpuscle to change shape again. In the context of individual differences that result in performance differences, some individuals may have more sensory receptors than others, and some individuals' sensory receptors may respond to relatively weak stimuli, while others' sensory receptors may require more intense stimulation before they fire.

Action on Other Neurons

A neuron affects other neurons by releasing a neurotransmitter that binds to chemical receptors. The effect upon the postsynaptic neuron is determined not by the presynaptic neuron or neurotransmitter, but by the type of receptor on the postsynaptic neuron that's activated. A neurotransmitter can be thought of as a key and a receptor as a lock; however, the same type of key can be used to open many different types of locks. As with neurons, synaptic receptors can be broadly classified as excitatory (causing an increase in firing rate), inhibitory (causing a decrease in firing rate), or modulatory (causing long-lasting effects not directly related to firing rate).

The two most common neurotransmitters in the brain, glutamate and Gamma-aminobutyric Acid (GABA), have actions that are largely consistent. Glutamate acts on several different types of receptors, and has the effect of being excitatory at ionotropic (ionotropic receptors are a group of <u>transmembrane</u> <u>ion-channel</u> proteins that open to allow ions to pass through the membrane in response to the binding of a chemical messenger, such as a neurotransmitter) receptors and modulatory at metabotropic (indirectly linked with ion channels on the plasma membrane of the cell through signal-transduction mechanisms) receptors. Gamma-aminobutyric Acid also has an effect on several different types of receptors, but it differs from glutamate in that the GABA effect is always inhibitory. Because of this consistency, it is common for neuroscientists to simplify the terminology by referring to cells that release glutamate as "excitatory neurons," and to cells that release GABA as "inhibitory neurons." Since over 90% of the neurons in the brain release either glutamate or GABA, these labels are applicable to most of them.

There are also other types of neurons that have consistent effects on their targets. For example, "excitatory" neurons are motor neurons in the spinal cord that release acetylcholine, and "inhibitory" spinal neurons release glycine.

The distinction between excitatory and inhibitory neurotransmitters is not absolute, but as indicated above, it depends on the class of chemical receptors present on the postsynaptic neuron. In principle, a single neuron, releasing a single neurotransmitter, can have excitatory effects on some targets, inhibitory effects on others, and modulatory effects on others, still.

For example, in the absence of light, photoreceptor cells in the retina constantly release the neurotransmitter glutamate. Some cells referred to as "OFF" bipolar cells are excited by the released glutamate, while neighbouring target neurons, called "ON" bipolar cells, are inhibited by the released glutamate. (The "ON" bipolar cells lack the typical ionotropic glutamate receptors and instead have inhibitory metabotropic glutamate receptors.) When light strikes the retina, the photoreceptors cease releasing glutamate, and this relieves the "ON" bipolar cells from inhibition, thus activating them. At the same time, the presence of light stops the excitation from the "OFF" bipolar cells, silencing them. As a result of this type of structure, a rapid bit type of response is generated by the photoreceptor cells in the retina.

Classification by Neurotransmitter

Another way of differentiating neurons is by the type of neurotransmitter they produce. Some examples of neurons based on the type of produced neurotransmitters are:

- **Cholinergic neurons** (Transmitter: acetylcholine). Cholinergic neurons provide the primary source of acetylcholine to the cerebral cortex and are known for their role in promoting cortical activation during both wakefulness and rapid eye movement (REM) sleep. In recent years, the cholinergic system of neurons has been a main focus of research in aging and neural degradation, specifically as it relates to Alzheimer's disease. In addition, it is known that the dysfunction and loss of basal forebrain cholinergic neurons and their cortical projections are among the earliest pathological events in Alzheimer's disease. (http://en.wikipedia.org/wiki/Cholinergic_neuron#cite_note-Nyakas-3, 2014/03/14)

- **Glutamatergic neurons** (Transmitter: glutamate). Glutamate is one of two primary excitatory amino acids, the other being aspartate. Glutamate receptors fall into four categories, three of which are chemically gated ion channels and one of which is a G-protein coupled receptor (often referred to as GPCR). AMPA and kainate receptors are chemically gated ion channels that mediate fast excitatory synaptic transmission. NMDA receptors are chemically gated ion channels that are more permeable to Ca2+ ions. And metabotropic receptors (the GPCRs) modulate synaptic transmission and postsynaptic excitability.

- **Dopaminergic neurons** (transmitter: dopamine). Dopamine is connected to mood and behaviour, and it modulates both pre and post-synaptic neurotransmission. Loss of dopamine neurons in the substantia nigra has been linked to Parkinson's disease.

- **Serotonergic neurons** (Transmitter: serotonin). Serotonin has been linked to depression. Drugs such as Prozac and Zoloft that block the presynaptic serotonin transporter are used in the treatment of depression.

Endorphins
(http://en.wikipedia.org/wiki/Endorphins)

Endorphins ("endogenous morphine") are endogenous (occurring naturally within the body) opioid peptides that function as inhibitory neurotransmitters. They are produced by the pituitary gland and the hypothalamus in vertebrates as a result of causative agents such as exercise, excitement, pain, consumption of spicy foods, and intercourse and other sexual activity. Endorphins resemble opiates in their abilities to produce analgesia and a feeling of well-being (euphoria).

Beta-endorphin (β-endorphin) is released into the blood from the pituitary gland and into the spinal cord and brain from hypothalamic neurons. β-endorphin has the highest affinity for the Mu 1 (μ1) opioid receptor, slightly lower affinity for the Mu 2 (μ2) and Delta (δ) opioid receptors, and low affinity for the Kappa 1 (κ1) opioid receptors. μ-Opioid receptors are the main receptor through which morphine acts. In the classical sense, μ-opioid receptors are presynaptic, and inhibit neurotransmitter release. Through this mechanism, they inhibit the release of the inhibitory neurotransmitter GABA, thus activating the dopamine pathways, causing more dopamine to be released. Opioid receptors have many important roles in the brain and periphery neurological structures including the modulation of pain, and cardiac, gastric, and vascular functions. Panic and satiation sensations may also be modulated by the action of opioid receptors.

> **Sidebar: Runner's High**
> A reputed effect of endorphins is the so-called "runner's high," which is said to occur when people exercise so strenuously that their bodies reach the threshold for endorphin release. The release of endorphins is thought to mitigate pain sensation by negatively regulating pain-carrying signals from nociceptive neurons in the spinal cord. This is referred to as an "analgesic" (pain-reduction) effect, and in addition to it, the runner's high has also been associated with feelings of euphoria.
> The analgesic effects of endorphins may also contribute to injuries, because as the pain sensation in the body is reduced, it becomes possible to push the body beyond its physical limits, thereby increasing the possibility of a person injuring themselves. (http://en.wikipedia.org/wiki/Endorphins, 3.1 Runner's High)

Number of Neurons in the Brain

The number of neurons in the brain varies dramatically from species to species. One estimate puts the human brain at about 100 billion (10^{11}) neurons and 100 trillion (10^{14}) synapses. A lower 2012 estimate is 86 billion neurons, of which 16.3 billion are in the cerebral cortex, and 69 billion in the cerebellum. By contrast, the nematode worm (*Caenorhabditis Elegans*) has just 302 neurons, and the fruit fly (*Drosophila Melanogaster*), a common subject for biological research, approximately 100,000 neurons.

Many properties of neurons, like the type of neurotransmitter mediating synaptic transmission and the composition of the ion channel, are consistent across species. This enables researchers to use a simple organism such as the fruit fly to study and understand processes occurring in more complex organisms such as human beings.

Neurons and Drugs

Many drugs act on the body by interacting with neuro receptors. The drugs are typically introduced in some fashion (inhaling, imbibing, injecting) into the blood stream. They are then carried throughout the body where they will cause their characteristic effects. Many of the popular recreational-type drugs have their primary effect on receptors in the brain.

Nicotine
(http://thebrain.mcgill.ca/flash/i/i_03/i_03_m/i_03_m_par/i_03_m_par_nicotine.html#drogues)

Nicotine imitates the action of a natural neurotransmitter called acetylcholine and binds to a particular type of acetylcholine receptor known as the nicotinic receptor. Whether it is acetylcholine or nicotine that binds to this receptor, it responds in the same way: it changes its conformation, which causes its associated ion channels to open for a few milliseconds. This channel then allows sodium ions to enter the neuron, depolarizing the membrane and exciting the cell. Then the channel closes again, and the nicotinic receptor becomes temporarily unresponsive to any neurotransmitters. It is this state of desensitization (basically a sedative effect) that is artificially prolonged by continual exposure to nicotine.

Opiates (Heroin)
(http://thebrain.mcgill.ca/flash/i/i_03/i_03_m/i_03_m_par/i_03_m_par_heroine.html#drogues)

As mentioned in the discussion of endorphins, the human body produces its own opiate-like substances and uses them as neurotransmitters. These substances include endorphins, enkephalins, and dynorphins, and are often collectively known as endogenous opioids. Endogenous opioids modulate our reactions to painful stimuli.

They also regulate vital functions such as hunger and thirst and are involved in mood control, immune response, and other processes.

The reason that opiates such as heroin and morphine affect us so powerfully is that these exogenous substances bind to the same receptors as our endogenous opioids. These receptors, through second messengers, influence the likelihood that ion channels will open, which in certain cases reduces the excitability of the affected neurons. This reduced excitability is the likely source of the euphoric effect of opiates.

This euphoric effect also appears to involve another mechanism in which the GABA-inhibitory interneurons of the ventral tegmental area come into play. By attaching to their Mu (μ) receptors, exogenous opioids reduce the amount of GABA released. Normally, GABA reduces the amount of dopamine released in the nucleus accumbens. By reducing this inhibitor, the opiates ultimately increase the amount of dopamine produced, which results in an increased sense of pleasure.

Chronic consumption of opiates inhibits the production of cAMP, and this inhibition is offset, in the long run, by other cAMP-production mechanisms. When no opiates are available, the increased cAMP production capacity comes to the fore and results in neural hyperactivity and the sensation of craving the drug.

Caffeine
(http://thebrain.mcgill.ca/flash/i/i_03/i_03_m/i_03_m_par/i_03_m_par_cafeine.html#drogues)

It is believed that caffeine (coffee, tea, and other caffeinated beverages) is consumed on a daily basis by 90% of all adults in the US. The stimulant effect of caffeine comes largely from the way it acts on the adenosine receptors in the neural membrane. When adenosine binds to its receptors, neural activity slows down, and the person feels sleepy. Adenosine thus facilitates sleep and dilates the blood vessels, possibly to ensure good oxygenation of the blood while sleeping.

Caffeine acts as an adenosine-receptor antagonist. This means that it binds to the same receptors, but without reducing neural activity. Fewer receptors are thus available to the natural "braking" action of adenosine, and neural activity therefore speeds up.

The activation of numerous neural circuits by caffeine also causes the pituitary gland to secrete hormones that in turn cause the adrenal glands to produce more adrenalin. Adrenalin is the "fight-or-flight" hormone, so it increases attention levels and gives the entire system an extra burst of energy. This is exactly the effect that many coffee drinkers are looking for.

In general, every cup of coffee has a stimulating effect, and any tolerance that may build up is likely to be minimal. However, caffeine may also create a physical dependency. Like many psychoactive drugs, caffeine increases the production of dopamine in the brain's pleasure circuits, thus helping to maintain the dependency on it. The symptoms of withdrawal from caffeine typically begin within one or two days after consumption ceases and can affect one out of every two individuals. Withdrawal symptoms typically include headaches, nausea, and sleepiness.

Types of Neurons

When neurons connect to each other, they are said to form neural networks. There are a number of special types of neurons that are formed together to make up a number of neural networks:

Sensory neurons respond to sensations (sound, light, pressure, etc.) received by the sensory organs (eyes, ears, nose, tongue, skin, etc.) that send signals via the spinal cord to the brain.

Motor neurons receive signals from the brain and spinal cord, and then enervate muscle and/or affect glands.

Interneurons connect neurons to other neurons within the same region of the brain or spinal cord.

Neural Coding

There are no pictures stored in the brain. Images are not saved in the same way that we see our reflection in a mirror. Sounds are not recorded in the same way that we hear an echo. Smells are not saved by trapping a compound and locking it in the brain, and muscles are not made to move by pulling a cord in the brain. Everything that happens through the nervous system and in the brain is coded, transmitted, effected, and stored in a fashion that is more like the coding used in computers than any physical aspect of the world we experience.

As discussed, a neuron essentially provides an "all-or-none" response. The Pacinian corpuscles provide a signal when depressed and a signal when released. If there is no change in pressure, then no signal is produced. This is similar to a simple on/off switch. It has also been noted that a nerve may have a varying rate of response. A high rate of response (high frequency) may represent a frequency of light at high intensity, and a lower rate of response (low frequency) may represent the same frequency of light at a lower intensity. As mentioned in the discussion of photoreceptors in the retina, a single receptor is limited in the type of signal it can generate and the amount of information it can convey. But by combining the actions of two receptors, it is possible to generate a more refined signal that can be used to transmit more information. Similarly, the more receptors that are connected and the more neurons that are combined increase the amount and quality of the information that can be transmitted and stored.

The manner in which the brain actually parses (breaks into smaller parts) information and transmits it along neurons, nerves, and neuronal pathways, and then processes it or stores it in various structures, or uses it to affect some physical action, is referred to as neural coding.

Common Neuronal Pathways

The following information presents a very limited perspective of the total amount of knowledge that exists on neuronal pathways. This limited perspective is presented in order to raise awareness and to give the reader an impression of the sophistication of the neural systems that have evolved. As mentioned previously, these systems are not unique to humans; they are also present in other animals. The reader is advised that the information presented here has (to the largest extent) been extracted from Wikipedia. It's very limited, and the reader is encouraged to seek out more in-depth and complete information.

Visual System

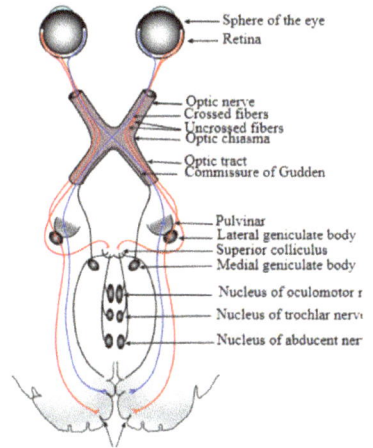

Image 7, Visual System

The visual system is the component of the central nervous system that gives organisms the ability to process visual detail and enables the formation of several non-image photo response functions. It detects and interprets information from visible light to build a representation of the surrounding environment. The visual system carries out a number of complex tasks, including the reception of light, the formation of monocular representations, the buildup of a nuclear binocular perception from a pair of two-dimensional projections, the identification and categorization of visual objects, the assessment of distances between objects, and the guiding of body movements in relation to visual objects. The physiological processing of visual information is known as visual perception, and a lack of that is called blindness. Non-image-forming visual functions, independent of visual perception, include the pupillary light reflex (PLR) and circadian photo-entrainment. (http://en.wikipedia.org/wiki/Visual_system, 2015/04/24)

Auditory System

While not part of the nervous system, the components of the outer ear feed into that part of the nervous system that performs the mechanical-electrical transduction of sound pressure waves into neural action potentials.

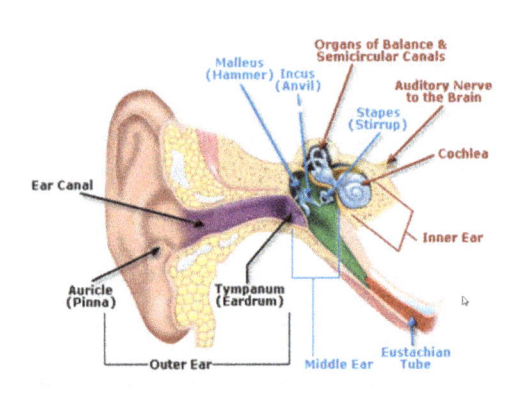

Image 8, Human Inner Ear
Attribution: Occupational Safety & Health Administration (1999). Section III: Health Hazards. Chapter 5: Noise.

Sound waves collect in the outer ear and then enter the auditory canal. The auditory canal amplifies sounds that are in the 3 to 12 kHz range. At the far end of the ear canal is the tympanic membrane, which marks the beginning of the middle ear. The sound waves strike the tympanic membrane (eardrum), and, through the mechanical processes of the middle ear, are converted from lower-pressure vibrations to higher-pressure sound vibrations at another, smaller membrane called the oval (or elliptical) window. Higher pressure is necessary at the oval window because the inner ear beyond the oval window contains liquid rather than air, and the sound waves are then being propagated in the fluid medium.

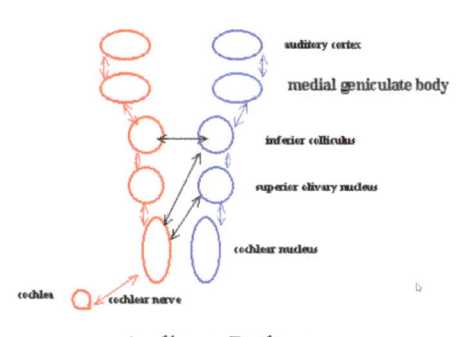

BRAIN PHYSIOLOGY

Inside the cochlea is a ribbon of hair-lined tissue referred to as the organ of Corti. It is in the hair cells of the organ of Corti that the fluid waves are converted to nerve signals. The neurotransmitter glutamate mediates the transfer of the signal from the hair cells to the dendrites of the primary auditory neurons, which, in turn, join the vestibular nerve to form the vestibulocochlear nerve. The signal then travels down the vestibulocochlear nerve, through intermediate stations such as the cochlear nuclei, the superior olivary complex of the brainstem, and the inferior colliculus of the midbrain, receiving further processing at each step in the pathway. The auditory information eventually reaches the thalamus, and from there it is relayed to the auditory cortex. (http://en.wikipedia.org/wiki/Auditory_system)

Auditory Pathway

Image 9, Auditory Pathway

Olfactory System

The olfactory system is the sensory system used for the sense of smell. Most mammals and reptiles have two distinct parts to their olfactory system: a main olfactory system, which detects volatile, airborne substances that are inhaled

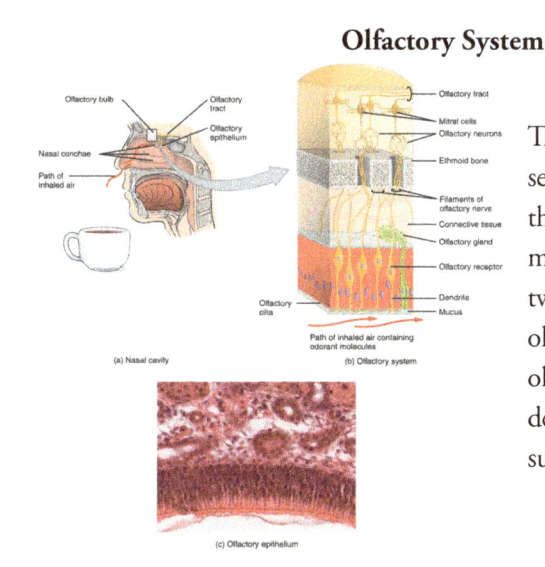

Image 10, Olfactory System

through the nose; and an accessory olfactory system, which may be functional in detecting pheromones.

The olfactory system is a chemosensory system that converts chemical stimuli into nerve signals. The signals travel along the olfactory nerve, which terminates in the olfactory bulb. Inside the olfactory bulb, axons connect with dendrites of mitral cells as well as other types of cells, and through the mitral cells, signals are sent to a number of other areas of the brain including the anterior olfactory nucleus, piriform cortex, medial amygdala, entorhinal cortex, and olfactory tubercle.

An interesting aspect of these connections is the one with the amygdala, which has been associated with attaching emotional tags to memories. Research has shown that odours can be a strong stimulus for triggering various memories. In addition to contributing emotional tags to memories, the amygdala has also been shown to be involved in social functions such as mating. http://en.wikipedia.org/wiki/Olfactory_system

Gustatory System

Gustatory is another word for "taste." Like smell, taste is a form of chemoreception that occurs in specialized receptors in the mouth. These receptors are known as taste cells, and they are contained in bundles called taste buds, which exist in the raised areas known as papillae found across the tongue. Previously, it was accepted that there were four primary tastes, but a current argument is being made for the recognition of five primary tastes: salt, sweet, sour, bitter, and umami. http://en.wikipedia.org/wiki/Gustatory_system

Taste occurs as a result of food dissolved in saliva coming into contact with taste receptors. A chemical reaction within the taste receptor creates an action potential that results in signals being transmitted via the seventh, ninth, and tenth cranial nerves to the gustatory areas of the brain. http://en.wikipedia.org/wiki/Taste_bud

Neural Systems in Review

From a psychological perspective, what is the significance of knowing that these pathways exist and how they function?

In each individual, the receptor cells and operational mechanisms vary slightly within certain biological parameters. This results in perceptions and experiences that vary from individual to individual. For some, there's a vast array of vibrant colours; for others, it is a dull world of colours that lack a range of hues or even no sight at all. This range of perceptual differences produces utterly unique experiences of the world.

Imagine two people standing in a park, looking around, listening to the sounds, and breathing in the fresh air. These individuals will be having two totally unique experiences thanks to their unique sensory filters and the way they drive their attention to focus on different aspects of the park. While one person's sensory experience may drive them to focus on sights and sounds, another's may cause them to focus on smells and internal emotional responses. They will sense and remember different things, and this reality will impart different memories, feelings, and emotions of the park experience. So, these two individuals, standing together in a park, will have totally different experiences of their surroundings that result in very different perceptions and understandings of the world.

Brain Structure and Function

The human brain is an extraordinarily complex organ. Through research and study, scientists have been able to identify functionally specific regions in the brain. Chemical molecules and electrical impulses constantly flow through and between these regions, sending signals and messages to other parts of the brain and body that result in physical responses, experiences, and thoughts.

At a high level, the brain is composed of the following functional structures:

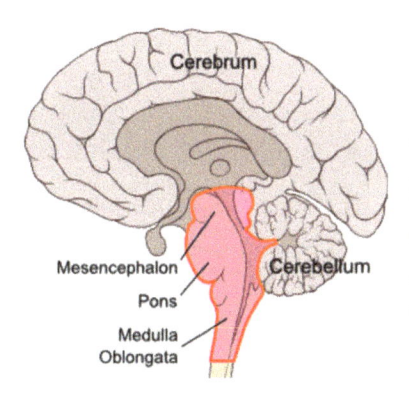

Image 11, Brainstem
Attribution: Patrick J. Lynch, variation by User:Hk kng

Brainstem

The brainstem connects the brain to the nerves in the spinal cord. It is the centre for basic life support: breathing, beating of the heart, waking, and sleeping.

Cerebellum

The cerebellum is connected to the brainstem at the back of the skull. It is tasked with coordinating body movements, controlling posture, and maintaining equilibrium.

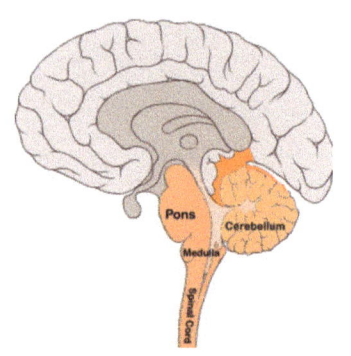

Image 12, Cerebellum Attribution:Patrick J. Lynch, medical illustrator; C. Carl Jaffe, MD, cardiologist.

Limbic System

The limbic system is composed of several structures that make up what is often referred to as the old mammalian brain because it is a structure that we have in common with other mammals.

The limbic system is responsible for maintaining the balance of the body's internal functions: temperature, blood pressure, sugar levels, etc. It also regulates emotions and the powerful drives of self-preservation and sexual desire. The four most important parts of the limbic system are the amygdala, the hippocampus, the hypothalamus, and the thalamus.

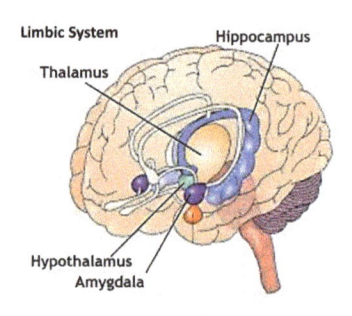

Image 13, Limbic System

- The amygdala is the pathway into the limbic system for sensory impulses.

- The hippocampus is a basic information processor. It matches new information with information that's already stored in the brain. The hippocampus plays an important role in consolidating information from short-term memory into long-term memory.

Because both sides of the brain are symmetrical, the hippocampus can be found in both hemispheres, and it has been found that if one side of the hippocampus is damaged or destroyed, memory function will remain nearly normal as long as the other side is undamaged. Damage to both sides of the hippocampus can impede the ability to form new memories; this is referred to as anterograde amnesia.

The functioning of the hippocampus can also decline with age. By the time people reach their eighties, they may have lost as much as 20% of the nerve connections in the hippocampus. While not all older adults exhibit this neuron loss, those who do so show decreased performance on memory tests. (http://psychology.about.com/od/memory/ss/ten-facts-about-memory_2.htm)

The hypothalamus acts as a liaison between the body and the rest of the brain. It releases at least seven different hormones to the pituitary gland, which, in turn, releases hormones into the bloodstream, influencing growth and sex.

- The thalamus is a relay station, sending signals from the rest of the body to the appropriate regions of the brain.

Cerebrum

The cerebrum surrounds the limbic system. In humans, the cerebrum is the largest part of the brain. It is here that nerve impulses get translated into images, symbols, words, and ideas. The cerebrum is divided into two halves, or cerebral hemispheres (left and right cerebral hemispheres), connected by the corpus callosum.

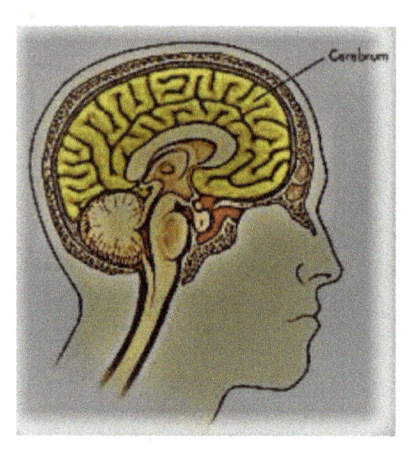

Image 14, Cerebrum Attribution: © William Fehr

Corpus Callosum

The corpus callosum is composed of millions of nerve fibres that act as a conduit for messages traveling between the right and left cerebral hemispheres. It is damage in this part of the brain that leads to the intriguing scenarios seen in split-brain research.

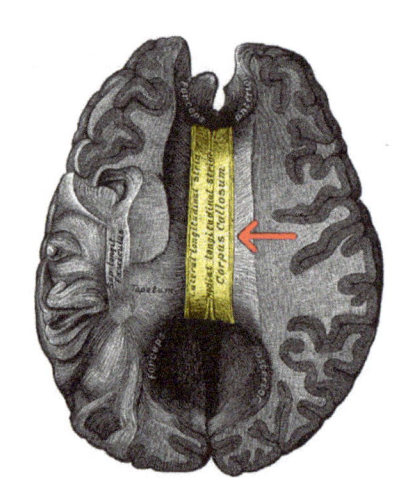

Image 15, Corpus Callosum
Attribution: Henry Vandyke Carter

Cortex

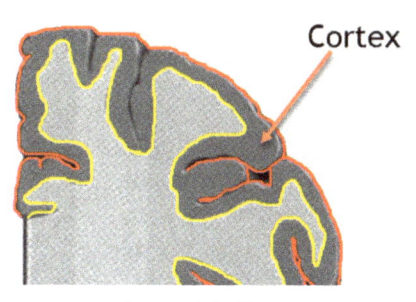

Image 16, Cortex
Attribution: By Grook Da Oger

The cortex is the convoluted surface with which we generally associate the brain. The cortex overlays the cerebrum and it is the centre of conscious thought and perception. In addition, it manages the integration of all sensation and responses. The cortex is the most recently evolved structure in the brain. It is also the most developed in humans and is considered the centre for the highest levels of functioning within the human brain.

Cerebral Cortex

To further the knowledge of brain anatomy, the following 3D rendition of Brodmann areas is shown. The diagram has been overlaid with labels to indicate the approximate locations of some of the more notable brain functions.

Brodmann areas were originally defined and numbered by the German anatomist Korbinian Brodmann. He used the Nissl method of cell staining and published his maps of cortical areas in 1909. Brodmann tabled more than fifty areas of the brain based on his research involving humans, monkeys, and other species. (2015-04-25, http://en.wikipedia.org/wiki/Brodmann_area). More recent research is expected to document between 100 and 200 distinct areas of the brain. (20150425, http://www.technologyreview.com/featuredstory/526501/brain-mapping/)

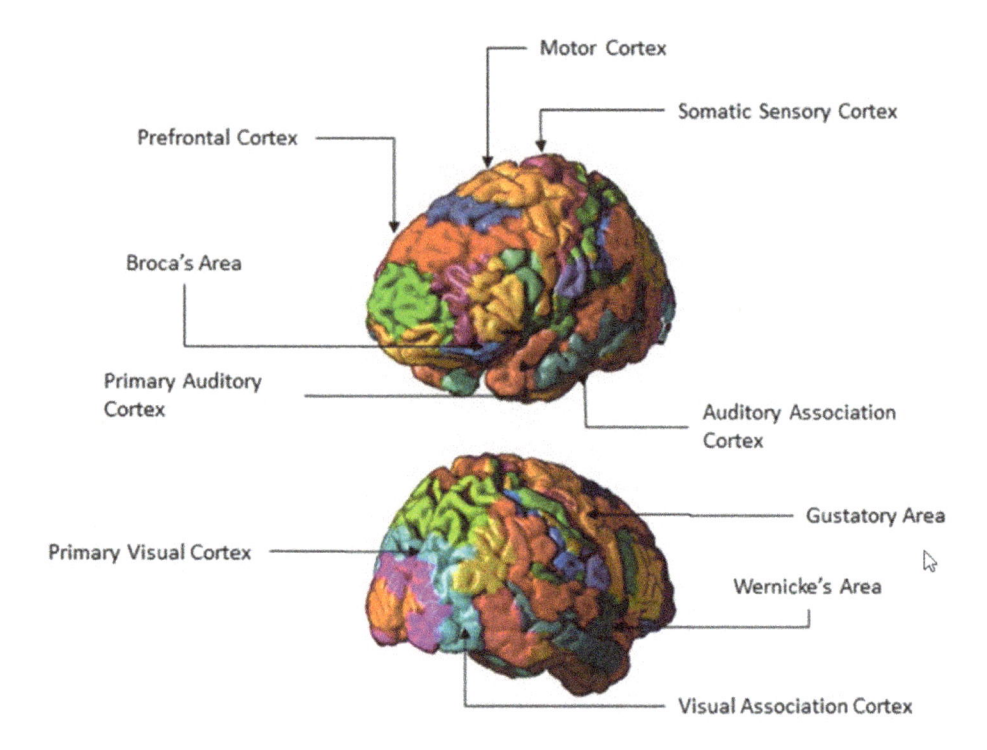

Image 17, Functional Areas of the Brain

(Kotulak, 1996, 1997, p.10)

- Motor cortex: The region of the cerebral cortex involved in the planning, control, and execution of voluntary movements.

- Prefrontal cortex: Many authors have indicated an integral link between a person's personality and the functions of the prefrontal cortex. This brain region has been implicated in planning complex cognitive behaviour, personality expression, decision-making, and moderating social behaviour. The basic activity of this brain region is considered to be orchestration of thoughts and actions in accordance with internal goals. (20150425, http://en.wikipedia.org/wiki/Prefrontal_cortex)

- Broca's area: An area of the brain that has been linked to language processing and speech.

- Primary auditory cortex: This region detects qualities of sounds such as tones and loudness and processes auditory information.

- Wernicke's area: This region is involved in the production of written and spoken language. (2015-04-25, http://en.wikipedia.org/wiki/Wernicke%27s_area)

- Somatic sensory cortex: This is the main sensory receptive area for the sense of touch.

- Visual association cortex: Cells in this area are involved in simple properties such as orientation, spatial frequency, and colour. (2015-04-25, http://en.wikipedia.org/wiki/Visual_cortex#V2)

- Primary visual cortex: Both hemispheres of the brain contain a visual cortex. The left hemisphere visual cortex receives signals from the right visual field, and the right visual cortex receives signals from the left visual field. This area of the brain transmits information to two primary pathways known as the ventral and dorsal streams. The ventral stream is associated with form recognition and object representation. It is also associated with the storage of long-term memory. The dorsal stream is associated with motion, representation of object locations, and control of the eyes and arms. (2015-04-25, http://dictionary.reference.com/browse/saccades%20?s=t)

- Gustatory area: This is a brain structure responsible for the perception of taste.

Brain Development

According to Ronal Kotulak, billions of brain cells are formed in the first months of fetal life. About half of them die off as hormones and other stimuli eliminate and organize the cells to form the brain's basic structures and attributes. After birth, trillions of connections are established and the various neuronal pathways (hearing, vision, touch, taste, etc.) become refined. From ages four to ten, rapid learning occurs; new connections continue to be formed, along with a considerable amount of reorganization. After age ten, the amount of reorganization starts to diminish, but the individual continues to learn and develop new memories, and new connections continue to develop in conjunction with this activity. (Chicago Tribune/Steve Little, Terry Volpp)

The Unique Brain

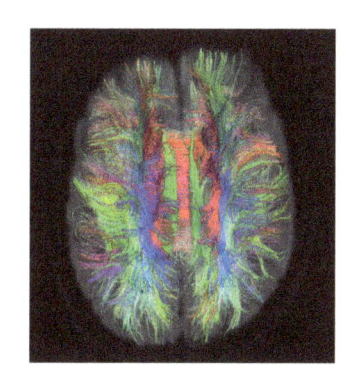

Image 18, Finger Print

Image 19, Brain MRI (Ruopeng Wang, The Athinoula A. Martinos Center for Biomedical Imaging at Massachusetts General Hospital)

Consider again the diagrams of the fingerprint and the brain MRI (above). Note that the fingerprint is recognizable by such aspects as the characteristic loops and swirls and the particular flow to the lines that form a pattern. As with the fingerprint, every brain presents a common structure: the brain stem, cerebellum, amygdala, corpus callosum, cerebrum, cortex, etc. Also like the fingerprint, each person's brain is unique to that individual. As has been described in the preceding discussion, even though healthy brains share a set of common structures with common functions, the actual composition of those structures is unique, and that individuality manifests itself in many performance differences, individual talents, and aptitudes.

In review, it is apparent that the physiological functioning of the nervous system and brain is well understood. It is also apparent that there are many aspects of neuronal functioning that will result in variable human performance, For example:

- The speed that a signal travels along a neuron can vary, resulting in some individuals having neurons that convey signals more rapidly than others (faster reflexes).

- For some individuals, neurons may have faster release rates for a neuro-transmitter mediating what may be interpreted as a more intense response (better learning, vision, hearing; more intense emotions; etc.).

- An individual may end up with a higher concentration of neuro-transmitters in the synaptic gap mediating a difference in the "all-or-none" response (a signal that reaches the critical level to generate an action potentiation in one individual may not reach that same level in someone else; if it doesn't, the signal will be lost and it will be as if there was no stimulus to begin with).

- Some individuals may produce greater concentrations of inhibitory neuro-transmitters and, thus, the strength of the signal may be suppressed or lost (higher tolerance to pain).

- Individuals for whom the intensity of a signal or message is greater may have stronger memories or experience faster learning.

- Individuals with higher concentrations of modulator neuro-transmitters may enjoy greater control of neuronal responses leading to greater control within their nervous system, which may also result in greater muscle control (coordination).

Indeed, there is a vast number of ways differential functioning in the nervous system can result in differential performance in individuals and define those differences. All of these are physiological differences that are primarily determined by genetics, developed in utero, refined in early childhood, and prove to be very stable over time.

In short, the brain is an exceedingly large and complex memory and messaging network that is unique to each individual. All feelings, senses, awareness, actions, thoughts, and, in effect, human consciousness are primarily mediated by an electro-chemical messaging process, and that process is fast enough to provide what is experienced as a continuous (uninterrupted) consciousness.

Feelings and Emotions

As surprising as it may seem to some, it appears that among the more significant core functions in our brain is the one responsible for feelings or emotions. In addition to decoding and giving significance to sensory information, the emotional function of the brain is also involved in memory, motivation, decision-making, and possibly more.

Hand Exercise

In order to get a sense of both how purposeful feelings are in our lives and how very subtle those that direct our lives can be, try this simple experiment:

Image20, Hands, Left over Right
Image created by author: Dr Dennis Wilson, PhD.

Image 21, Hands, Right over Left
Image created by author: Dr Dennis Wilson, PhD.

Place your hands together, interlocking your fingers. Look at your thumbs. One of the thumbs—either the left or right—will be on the top. This can be referred to as the "natural position."

Now, switch your hands around interlocking your fingers so that the other thumb is on top. This can be referred to as the "unnatural position."

How does it feel? It probably feels a little awkward. It is this simple and subtle feeling that keeps us consistently interlocking our hands together with the thumbs in the "natural position" as opposed to the "unnatural position." For some, the "natural position" may be with the left thumb on top, and for others, the "natural position" may be with the right thumb on top.

It may be said that there is a preference for placing our hands together with the thumbs in the natural position. At the same time, an individual can choose to put their hands together with the thumbs in the unnatural position, but it will feel uncomfortable, and it will continue to feel so unless it is practiced to the point at which it becomes second nature. However, regardless of how much practice is applied to placing the hands together with the thumbs in the unnatural position, there will always be a tendency to put the hands together with the thumbs in the natural position. The continuous performance of placing the thumbs in the unnatural position requires constant vigilance, an action that consumes energy and will cause an individual fatigue. It is fatigue at a very subtle level, but unnatural behaviour does require more effort and energy than following the natural tendency.

Also, it should be noted that, if the hands are in the natural position, there is typically no perceptible feeling at all. It's not that there is an identifiable feeling or rightness; it simply does not feel wrong. At a very subtle unconscious level, the individual knows that the reverse feels wrong, and so continues to put their hands together in the way that does not feel wrong—with the thumbs in the natural position. When the thumbs are in the natural position it feels comfortable, unnoticeable, and it is definitely not the same as the feeling of discomfort experienced when something is out of the ordinary. In other words, it may be that individuals continue with the unconscious perspective that all things are as they should be because there is no conscious feeling of something unusual.

In this context, it appears that preferences are not necessarily about a person's ability to do something, because anyone can put their hands together with either thumb on top. It appears that an individual's preferences are reflective of very subtle feelings: a sense of comfort or discomfort, a lack of a sense of discomfort, a sense of rightness, a sense of pleasure, etc. Simply put, they're a product of nothing more profound than a casual feeling of rightness.

Preferences also have elements of effort and energy. In order to continually function in an unnatural manner requires more energy and effort, likely due to the extra vigilance this calls for. Functioning in the natural way is easier, and, in some cases, may be stimulating.

Another experiment that can help in understanding the importance of feelings in mental functions is as follows:

If I were to say, "two plus two equals three," how does that statement make you feel?

For most of us, there will be a very slight level of discomfort. However, for some, there will be an intense urge to shout, "that's not correct!"

Again, this is the type of feeling that occurs when an individual senses that something may not be right. The feeling is typically very, very subtle, but it may be enough to consistently dictate thoughts and behaviours. An individual believes they're right when they have a feeling of "rightness," and that they're wrong when they "feel" wrong. From the perspective of logical thought, when something doesn't make logical sense, it "feels" wrong.

It is feelings like these—feelings that are ever so subtle—that may cause humans to consistently behave in ways that are recognized as characteristic of who they are. It is feelings like these that may dictate how each individual will tend to do things time and again.

Emotions and Motivation

Emotions tend to be rather simple: either positive or negative. According to Izard & Malatesta, there may be relatively few pure emotions: happiness, surprise, sadness, anger, disgust, contempt, and fear (Izard & Malatesta, 1987, http://en.wikipedia.org/wiki/Discrete_emotion_theory). These elemental feelings appear to have universally recognizable facial expressions. Further, it appears that the richness of emotional expression may come from the possibility that the few simple core emotions can be combined, like primary colours, to produce a rich array of emotional expression. For example:

- Jealousy may be a mix of anger and sadness.
- Guilt may be a combination of enjoyment and fear.

Emotions are closely linked to actions. In the mammalian past, emotions caused our ancestors to respond differently to food than to predators. Emotions do not require reflection (higher thought processes). They encourage the individual to do something—whether it be to feed, fight, flee, or any of the other "f" functions.

Pain, Pleasure, and Motivation

The images below depict the pain and pleasure centres in the brain.

The Pleasure Centre

Current thought is that the sense of pleasure is primarily facilitated in the nucleus accumbens, though stimuli to other parts of the brain results in concordant experiences (i.e., the person will experience a sensation of pleasure, but will *simultaneously* think, feel and do other things).

http://thebrain.mcgill.ca/flash/i/i_03/i_03_cr/i_03_cr_que/i_03_cr_que.html

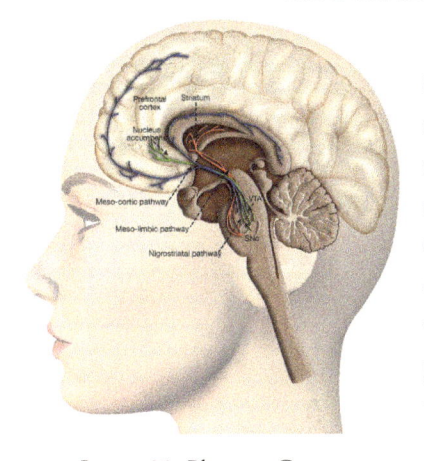

Image 22, Pleasure Centre Attribution: By Oscar Arias-Carrión, Xanic Caraza-Santiago, Sergio Salgado-Licona, Mohamed Salama, Sergio Machado, Antonio Egidio Nardi, Manuel Menéndez-González and Eric Murillo-Rodríguez.

Pain Centres

The experience of pain has a far more complex mapping in the brain than its counterpart, pleasure, as is depicted in the drawing to the right. This may explain the variety of thoughts and actions that occur in response to pain.

http://thebrain.mcgill.ca/flash/i/i_03/i_03_cr/i_03_cr_dou/i_03_cr_dou.html

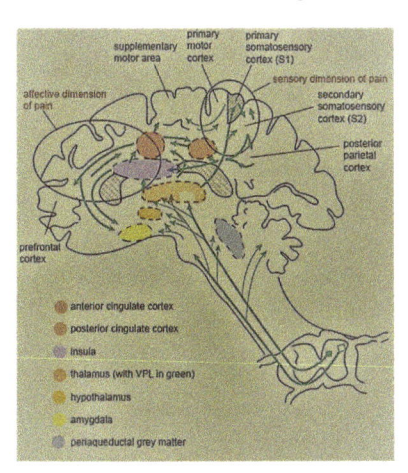

Image 23, Pain Centres Attribution: McGill University; Adapted from Price, D.D. (2000) Science Vol. 288, pp. 1769-1772

Motivation in Review

From a very basic perspective, individuals are fundamentally motivated to move toward pleasure and away from pain. A consideration of pain and pleasure should not be limited to only their physical strains, but should include their psychological strains, as well. For pain, this includes such things as the very subtle discomfort that causes an individual to do things consistently, like put the hands together in a certain fashion, along with fear, frustration, anxiety, disappointment, sadness, rejection, and so on.

When thinking of pleasure, the consideration should include such psychological examples as a sense of well-being or safety; and the experience of winning or having success, knowing something, feeling acceptance, and self-fulfillment.

Our efforts to understand and deal with people need to include a consideration of motivations, and the need to use the right motivator. Some things are motivational to some and not to others, such as carrot for the horse and the bone for the dog. The object used as a motivator needs to be appropriate to the entity/subject that is to be motivated.

Fear is a particularly strong motivator, and it's the one that many marketing campaigns are built on. Fear stimulants are often built into advertising, and a scare-you-into-buying method is commonly used to sell products, services, and even political leaders.

Decision-Making

It is theorized that the human brain relies on two processes in order to deal with the complexities of decision-making: "pattern recognition" and "emotional tagging." Both processes help the individual make decisions—most of the time. Research has indicated that even simple tasks, such as visual recognition, involve some thirty different parts of the brain. Each one focuses on a different type of input and looks for a memory of similar inputs that matches the current one. An integrating function then takes the information about what matches have been found, makes assumptions about missing bits of information, and arrives at a point of view. (<u>Think again why good leaders make bad decisions,</u> Finkelstein)

Finkelstein et al. goes on to say that individuals tag their thoughts and memories with the emotions they experience concurrently with an event. These emotional tags, when triggered by a pattern-recognition match, tell the individual whether to pay attention to something or ignore it, essentially providing them with an action orientation.

In addition to these processes/efforts in our decision-making, there also appears to be two channels through which the information is processed. LeDoux presents the theory that there is a sensory/thalamus "low road" to the amygdala and a sensory/cortex "high road" to the amygdala. The "low-road" path embodies a very rapid process with sensory input going in, getting processed, and very rapidly producing a response. The "high-road" path involves the sensory cortex along with extensive logical or mental processing at a higher level than emotion (feeling). Thought elements are subsequently fed into the amygdala, which produces an emotional (feeling) response.

Consider the low-road path as functional in the context of a baseball game, where the batter must hit a baseball travelling at anywhere between sixty and ninety miles an hour over a distance of sixty-and-a-half feet. In rounded figures, it would take between .46 and .69 of a second for the baseball to cover the distance between the pitcher's mound and home plate. The batter needs to watch the ball for a period of time to determine if it's a good pitch, make a decision, and make the swing. If we estimate that the batter watches the ball for between a half and two thirds the distance to the plate, depending on the speed of the ball, and then uses the remaining time to coordinate and make the swing, it would mean that the batter is processing the information and making the decision in roughly .23 of a second. This is definitely not a pathway with a lot of conscious cortical processing.

On the other hand, consider specifying the size of a steel beam to be used in the construction of a bridge. This is not a task that's typically left to, as is said, "eyeballing it." It's one that can typically require a significant amount of knowledge along with the ability to perform complex and detailed calculations. Engineering tasks are typical of those that require a great deal of cortical processing before a good decision can be made. Thus, it is reasonable to accept the premise that there is a "low road" and a "high road" to stimulus processing and decision-making.

In general, the performance of humans on any given task falls within certain performance limits, and it's typical for the total range of performance to be expressed by a bell curve, with the largest number of individuals appearing in the middle of the range and a diminishing number appearing near its limits. In addition, based on the physiological differences in the brain, it is reasonable to expect that some individuals will be more adept at low-road and some at high-road processing; some may be exceptional at both types, and some may not be very good at either.

This aspect of a "low road" and a "high road" for sensory input and processing aligns well with the theoretical model put forward by Ned Herrmann in the development of the Herrmann Brain Dominance Instrument©, where there is an upper and lower half to the model. In the model, the upper half is symbolic of the high road (more predominantly cortical) processing, and the lower half is symbolic of the low road (more predominantly emotional/feelings) processing. This same two-pathway concept may also be relevant to the postulation that some people are more analytical, and others are more empathetic. It also rings true in that the emotional processing is happening in the amygdala, where responses are triggered before moving to the appropriate action response site. This adds further support to the significance of the emotions or feelings aspect of decision-making, and the view of neural scientists that much of our mental processing is unconscious and that emotions (feelings) are essential to decision-making.

Along these lines, Wikipedia documented experiments in which participants were asked to identify whether certain nonsensical and made-up words belonged to word groupings they'd been shown previously. The experiments indicated that it might not be necessary to be consciously aware of grammatical rules to know proper grammar, which might explain people's sense that a certain sentence structure is awkward or wrong even though they can't say why.

Another dichotomy in decision-making was illustrated by Herbert A. Simon, who identified two cognitive styles as "maximizers" and "satisfiers." Maximizers are individuals who are inclined to try to make an optimal decision; satisfiers are individuals who tend to try to find a solution that's "good enough." It is further noted that maximizers tend to take longer making decisions, possibly due to their need to maximize performance across all variables and make tradeoffs carefully, and that they're more likely to regret their decisions (perhaps because they are more able than satisfiers to recognize that a decision turned out to be sub-optimal). (http://en.wikipedia.org/wiki/Decision-making.) The distinction between maximizers and satisfiers is understandable when the impact of potential physiological differences is considered.

An interesting piece of research that is possibly a little counterintuitive for some showed that, in situations with higher time pressures, stakes, or ambiguities, experts tended to use intuitive decision-making rather than structured approaches.

((http://en.wikipedia.org/wiki/Decision-making))

Why Decisions Go Wrong

In a general way, we have covered how the brain goes about making decisions; it employs basically two paths and relies heavily on the emotional/feelings aspect of brain function. Essentially, it appears as a relatively simple system that manages to handle very complex tasks. It should not be surprising that a simple system handling an extremely complex task would also be functionally flawed. Flawed functionality results in flawed decisions; Finkelstein et al. state that there are two factors at play in a flawed decision: an individual or group who has made an error in judgment and a decision process that fails to detect and correct the error. (Read *Think Again: Why Good Leaders Make Bad Decisions and How to Keep it From Happening to You,* by Sydney Finkelstein, Jo Whitehead, and Andrew Campbell (Feb 3 2009)). Finkelstein et al. go on to list the elements they've identified that can result in a flawed decision.

Misleading experiences

A misleading experience is a current experience that is very similar to a previous experience, except the current one includes a critical difference that is not identified. When we develop our sense of a situation, we align what we are experiencing in the present with similar aspects of a previous experience (matching). When our sense of the current situation tells us it's like a similar situation from the past, we reference the emotional tag associated with that situation's outcome. If the emotional tag on the outcome was positive, we'll respond with the same decision we did before. If the past situation's outcome was tagged with a negative emotion, we'll avoid making the same decision again.

In the context of misleading experiences, if the current situation is not *exactly* the same as the one in the past—indeed, if it differs in some critical way—then we may end up making a wrong decision.

Per Texas Hold 'Em

For illustrative purposes, consider how this would function in a game of Texas Hold 'Em.

Previously, a player won a hand when he was holding two jacks. This time, he is dealt two jacks again, and because he won with them in the past, he assumes he can again. Betting "all in" and playing out the hand may reveal that going whole hog with two jacks is not always a good bet.

Misleading Pre-judgments

A misleading pre-judgment takes place when a person makes an assumption about the significance of some aspect of a situation—and that assumption is incorrect. In other words, we may be aware of a number of elements of a situation but put a much greater emphasis on one of them over others. The emphasis on the one element may not be warranted, and we may make a decision based on this inappropriate focus. In this manner, pre-judgment can lead to flawed decisions.

Per Texas Hold 'Em

Again, consider how this might play. out in a game of Texas Hold 'Em.

Player A looks at Player B and decides Player B looks like a bit of a tricky player. On the deal, Player A receives a jack and a king, off suit; Player B receives two nines. Player A makes a strong bet and Player B calls the bet made by Player A. The flop comes and it's two jacks and a two. Player A now has three jacks, a king, and a two; Player B has two jacks, two nines, and a two. Player A makes another strong bet and Player B calls. On the turn, a nine is dealt. Player A makes another strong bet, and Player B, with a full house, nines over jacks, calls the bet. A five is dealt on the river, and Player A makes another strong bet; Player B raises it. Player A looks at the pair of jacks on the table and knows there's a chance that Player B may have a full house, but decides he's bluffing. So Player A raises again. Player B calls and wins the pot with a full house (nines over jacks) beating three jacks, a king, and a nine.

Inappropriate Self-interest

Inappropriate self-interest happens when an individual places a higher level of significance on aspects of a situation because they are of greater personal importance to the individual than others. For example, imagine a researcher who becomes much invested in his research project. As the project progresses, it becomes apparent that its results are not proceeding in the direction the researcher desires. Feeling personally invested in his perspective on the research, the researcher may turn to falsifying the data.

Per Texas Hold 'Em

If we consider this error in the context of Texas Hold 'Em, the situation would entail a player going many hands without having a winning hand, or even a hand of reasonably good cards. As time continues to pass and more hands are dealt, the player's stack of chips continues to diminish. In Texas Hold 'Em, there is a concept of "strength of the stack." Here, the more chips a player has, the greater is the strength of his stack; conversely, if the player is holding a relatively small value in chips, the strength of his stack is weak. The player needs to win some pots in order to maintain the strength of his/her stack. If the player has a diminishing strength in his/her stack he or she may feel some urgency to win a hand, and as a result he/she may try to force a winning hand. The need that a player feels for a winning hand does not mean his/her cards are going to improve. If the player succumbs to the feeling of urgency, and tries to force the situation, he/she may end up playing cards that are not good cards—cards they would normally play. Trying to force a winning hand by playing cards with a lower probability of winning may result in the player exiting the game more quickly.

Inappropriate attachments

Inappropriate attachments are similar to the attachment we might feel for colleagues or friends whose jobs we have to cut because of cost measures. Close friends and relatives tend to be hired and not to be fired, even in situations in which it would be appropriate to let them go.

Inappropriate attachment does not only apply to attachments with people, but also with objects, places, and events. A person may have a particular attachment to a house or a car and that can cause them to place an inappropriate or high value on it—more than the market is willing to pay. As a result, as much as the person may try to sell the article, the market rejects the personal valuation, and the article does not sell.

Per Texas Hold 'Em

In the context of Texas Hold 'Em, a player may have a particular affinity for suited cards, possibly because he thinks being dealt two cards of the same suit looks nice. This player may be inclined to bet the suited cards in hopes of making a flush. However, a liking for suited cards may extend well beyond the practical probability of making a winning flush hand. Betting the suited cards simply because you like the looks of them is not necessarily a good bet.

Controlling for Flawed Decisions

Research indicates that it is impractical for an individual to try and correct their mental processes. The brain's way of working (when it feels right, it simply feels right) makes the situation particularly difficult—hence, safeguards are recommended that are external to the individual. This reality highlights the advantage of working in partnerships, teams, and groups. Joining with people who have natural tendencies and talents that are more complementary than similar to your own tends to have a synergistic effect on the breadth and quality of the results.

In keeping with this concept, Herrmann International recommends "whole brain thinking." This is a process where a project group or team is constructed such that it contains at least one person who's dominant is each of the HBDI quadrants.

Another alternative that organizations use to improve decision-making and problem-solving is to turn to structured approaches. Structured decision-making is a general term for the carefully organized analysis of problems in order to reach decisions that are focused on achieving fundamental objectives. Structured Decision Making (SDM) is based in decision theory and risk analysis and encompasses a simple set of concepts and helpful steps. There are a number of variances in the implementation of SDM. The chart following presents a general form of the SDM process for making decisions based on clearly articulating fundamental objectives, dealing explicitly with uncertainty. Formulating the alternatives can include a broad range of considerations including legal aspects and public preferences and individual and group values.

In SDM, every decision consists of several primary elements: management objectives, decision options, and predictions of decision outcomes. By analyzing each component separately and thoughtfully within a comprehensive decision framework, it is possible to control for possible oversights or omissions, and the process improves the quality of decision-making. (http://www.fws.gov/science/doc/structured_decision_making_factsheet.pdf)

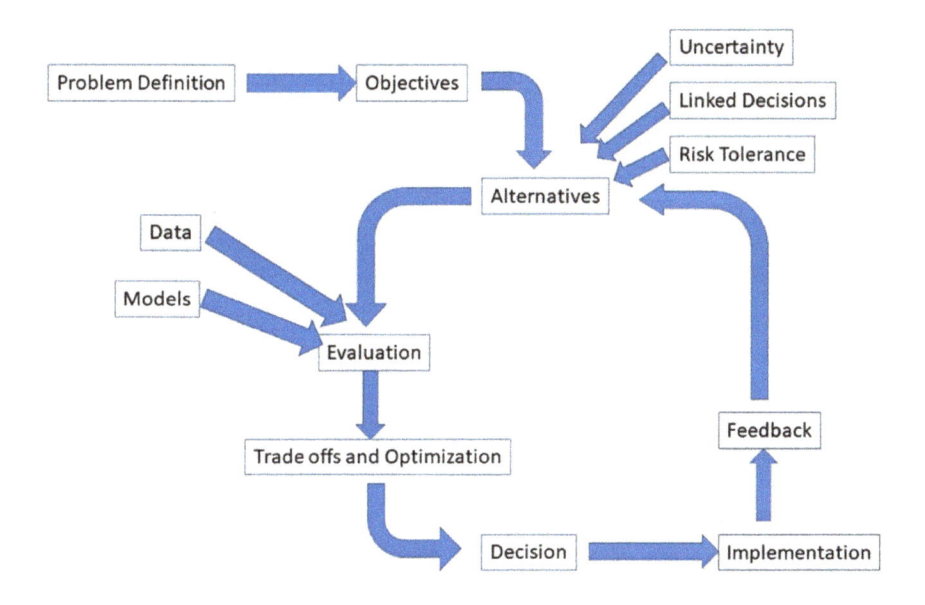

Figure 1, Structured Decision Method Process
Image created by the author: Dr. Dennis Wilson, PhD

The steps laid out in this SDM process are as follows:

Problem definition. What specific decision has to be made? What is the spatial and temporal scope of the decision? Will the decision be iterated over time?

Objectives. What are the management objectives? Ideally, these are stated in quantitative terms that relate to metrics that can be measured. Setting objectives falls in the realm of policy, and should be informed by legal and regulatory mandates, as well as stakeholder viewpoints. A number of methods for stakeholder elicitation and conflict resolution are appropriate for clarifying objectives.

Alternatives. What are the different management actions to choose from? This element requires explicit articulation of the alternatives available to the decision-maker. The range of permissible options is often constrained by legal or political considerations, but structured assessment may lead to creative new alternatives.

Evaluation. The evaluation needs to consider the consequences of different management actions? How many of the objectives would each alternative achieve? In formulating the alternatives there is a prediction of the consequences of the alternative actions. In general the alternatives are often expressed or represented in the form of models that can be empirically evaluated. Depending on the information available or the quantification desired for a structured decision process, consequences may be modeled with highly scientific computer applications or personal judgment elicited carefully and transparently. Ideally, models are quantitative, but they need not be; the important thing is that they link actions to consequences.

Tradeoffs. If there are multiple objectives, how do they trade off with each other? In most complex decisions, the best we can do is choose intelligently from among less-than-perfect alternatives. Numerous tools are available to help determine the relative importance or weighting among conflicting objectives and compare alternatives across multiple attributes to find the "best" compromise solutions.

Uncertainty. Because we rarely know precisely how management actions will affect natural systems, decisions are frequently made in the face of uncertainty. Uncertainty makes choosing among alternatives far more difficult. A good decision-making process will confront uncertainty explicitly and evaluate the likelihood of different outcomes and their possible consequences.

Risk tolerance. Identifying the uncertainty that impedes decision-making, then analyzing the risk that uncertainty presents to management, is an important step in making a good decision. Understanding the level of risk a decision-maker is willing to accept, or the risk response determined by law or policy, will make the decision-making process more objectives-driven, transparent, and defensible.

Linked decisions. Many important decisions are linked over time. The key to dealing effectively with linked decisions is to isolate and resolve the near-term issues while sequencing the collection of information needed for future decisions.

The core SDM concepts and steps to better decision-making are useful across all types of decisions: from individuals making minor or personal decisions to complex public-sector decisions involving multiple decision-makers, scientists, or other stakeholders.

All this is in recognition of the fact that the human brain has limitations and is not an infallible decision-making instrument.

Talents and Aptitudes

Talents are defined as: (1) "a special natural ability or aptitude;" (2) a capacity for achievement or success." (2015/04/26, http://dictionary.reference.com/browse/talent)

There is a video on YouTube (Youtube: https://www.youtube.com/watch?v=cPiDHXtM0VA) of an experiment conducted by Professor Tetsuro Matsuzawa at Kyoto University's Primate Research Institute in Japan. The video shows chimpanzees performing spatial memory tasks with a level of speed and accuracy that only a few exceptional humans can match. Does this mean chimpanzees are smarter than humans? No! It means that chimpanzees have some highly specialized brain functions, and that their brains are structured in a way that supports this type of specialized brain function. Thus, for this one particular type of task, this particular talent of chimpanzees demonstrates superior performance.

Similarly, even though each healthy human brain has the same basic structure, each human brain is unique. In no small part, the neurological differences discussed earlier contribute to each individual having brain functions that vary in speed, intensity, and duration. These mental differences, along with the physical attributes of the rest of our bodies, end up defining who we are, inherently, and how we relate to the world outside of our physical being.

Image 25, QR code for Split Brain Video

In another YouTube video (Utube file: http://www.youtube.com/watch?v=82tlVcq6E7A,) we follow Alan Alda as he is introduced to the research of Dr. Michael Gazzaniga (Dartmouth College, New Hampshire). The video portrays research involving a split-brain patient that demonstrates how the left and right hemispheres of the brain are highly specialized for specific functions. Among other things, this video illustrates that, if a brain structure is destroyed or damaged, the function supported by that brain structure either ceases or is impaired. It also implies that if the required synaptic connections do not exist, then neither will the thought.

Male and Female Differences

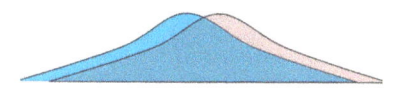

Image 26, Bi-modal Illustration
Image Created by the author; Dr. Dennis Wilson, PhD

As individuals, we are different, full stop. There are many identifiable differences in people. At a physical level, it is clear that males are different from females. In addition, there exists strong evidence that male brains are different from female brains—though not absolutely different. The difference can be understood and shown as a shift or slightly different skews in a bell curve for various mental functions.

If we were to measure the performance of humans on a given mental function and graph males and females separately, we might find that female performance would be represented as one bell curve and male performance another. When we overlay the two graphs, we might see that female and male performance are slightly offset. In this context, females and males, to the largest extent share the same performance range. In terms of physical performance, the difference is sufficient to justify separate sports leagues and categories in such athletic competitions as the Olympics. In terms of mental functioning, there may be a measurable difference in some functions, but whether one side of the bell-curve skew is more important than the other depends largely on what is being sought. In addition, any difference may not be relevant because of the extent of the overlap at the limits. In other words, if a hiring manager wanted to select for math ability, they may need to include both males and females in the selection process because, even though there may be a statistically significant difference between the sexes, the amount of overlap at the extremity suggests that either gender might be found to be the top performer.

The differences that we see and come to recognize in people, such as introversion and extroversion, are testament to very real differences in people. Differences are not necessarily good or bad or right or wrong. In fact, many aspects of life are improved when, as individuals, we can come to recognize, understand, and develop a respect for the differences. In addition, we need to adapt to deal with them.

Introverts and Extroverts

One of the first characteristic traits identified by philosophers and researchers attempting to understand human psychology was the dichotomy of introversion and extroversion. It has been argued that this is the easiest characteristic trait to identify in humans. There is considerable support for the view that the introversion and extroversion declaration is an indication of where and how the individual is energized.

Introverts

"Some popular psychologists have characterized introverts as people whose energy tends to expand through reflection and dwindle during interaction. This is similar to Jung's view, although he focused on mental energy rather than physical energy: "Mistaking introversion for shyness is a common error. Introverts have a preference for solitude over larger social activities, but introverts do not necessarily fear social encounters like shy people do." (5/10/2015, http://en.wikipedia.org/wiki/Extroversion_and_introversion)

Researchers using brain scans have found introverts have more brain activity in general, and specifically in the frontal lobes. When these areas are activated, introverts are energized. They are stimulated when their brains are involved in retrieving long-term memories, problem-solving, introspection, complex thinking, and planning (Introverted Youth have Deep Roots for Behaviour, MacGruder, USA). It has also been found that introverts will make faster and

63

better decisions in a quiet environment, or in an environment that provides less external stimulation.

Extroverts

"Extroverts are energized and thrive off being around other people. They take pleasure in activities that involve large social gatherings, such as parties, community activities, public demonstrations, and business or political groups. They also tend to work well in groups. An extroverted person is likely to enjoy time spent with people and find less reward in time spent alone. They tend to be energized when around other people, and they are more prone to boredom when they are by themselves." (5/10/2015, http://en.wikipedia.org/wiki/Extroversion_and_introversion)

Research has shown that extroverts have more activity in brain areas involved in processing sensory information. It may be theorized that because extroverts, in comparative terms, have less internally generated brain activity, they search for more external stimuli to energize themselves (McGruder, *USA Today*, November 28, 2005). Other research has found that extroverts will make faster and better decisions in a stimulating environment—one with lights, music, or other sensory inputs that stimulate and raise the extrovert to a higher level of awareness.

Reiterating for emphasis, to the best of researchers' theoretical understanding, the introversion/extroversion dichotomy is all about energy. Taking an extrovert out of their optimum environment and placing them in an alien environment—a sterile examination hall setting, for example—places them at a disadvantage. At the same time, a decision not to place introverts in upper-management positions because they are not socially gregarious (and may, in fact, be somewhat socially awkward) could end up eliminating some much-needed leadership and vital perspective within the upper echelons of an organization. It should be recognized that the best management does not come from winning a popularity contest.

Implications to Management

What great managers know

In 1999 Gallup poll introduced a book by Marcus Buckingham and Curt Coffman entitled *First, Break All The Rules: What The World's Greatest Managers Do Differently*. This work was built on the analysis of 80,000 managers across 400 companies.

According to Buckingham and Coffman, great managers don't believe that a person can achieve anything he sets his mind to with enough training, and so don't try to help people overcome their weaknesses. Great managers disregard the golden rule that everybody is equal—they will actually play favourites. What great managers know is that everybody is unique, and that people don't change much. They respect that uniqueness and bank on the consistency. Great managers know that it is a waste of time and money to try to develop talents in a person if the person is not already gifted with the talent. They should not try to make an individual something that they're not. Even with extensive training, it is not possible to turn a high-performing analytical type of person into a high-performing feeling type of person. Even with extensive training, it is not possible to turn the one into the other. Buckingham and Coffman argue that these are dichotomies that are diametrically opposed. The talents of one are quite different from the talents of the other. What is best, from the perspective of Buckingham and Coffman, is to try and draw out and hone the natural talents that each person already possesses.

Peter Drucker was a renowned writer, professor, management consultant and self-described "social ecologist." *Business Week* magazine referred to him as "the man who invented management." (http://www.druckerinstitute.com/peter-druckers-life-and-legacy/)

In Peter Drucker's opinion, it is more cost-effective and beneficial for the industry to try to take competent performers and make them stars than it is to try to take weak performers and make them into average performers. (Peter F. Drucker, *Management Challenges for the 21st Century*, Harper Business, 1999. 207 pages.)

The World's Simplest Management Secret
(Salesforce, Jeffrey James, October 24, 2012,
The World's Simplest Management Secret)

In his book, *The World's Simplest Management Secret*, Jeffrey James suggests that we forget what we've learned from management texts and remember that there is really only one way to ensure that everyone on your team excels. According to James, the management books have it all wrong in their efforts to instruct on how to manage people. It's impossible to manage people, he says, and argues it is only possible to manage individuals, because individuals are so different from one another; because of their unique brains. What works with one person may not work with another. Some people thrive on public praise while others feel uncomfortable when singled out. Some people are all about the money while others thrive on challenging assignments. Some people need mentoring while others find advice to be grating. The trick is to manage individuals as *they* want or need to be managed, not as *we* prefer to manage. The only way to do this is to understand the individual for who they are, not who we might like them to be (our preconceived notion or personal bias).

Psychometrics

Psychometrics is the field of study concerned with the theory and technique of educational and psychological measurement. It includes measurement of such elements as knowledge, aptitudes, abilities, attitudes, and behaviours. This field is primarily concerned with the construction and validation of measurement instruments such as questionnaires, tests, and various psychological assessments. It involves two major research tasks: the construction of instruments and procedures for measurement, and the development and refinement of theoretical approaches to measurement. (Wikipedia)

Validity and Reliability

The quality of a psychometric instrument is determined by its validity and reliability. The question of validity is: "Can we trust the instrument to do what it is intended to do?" If the instrument is promoted as a personality instrument, can we trust it to consistently provide the user with a personality profile? If the instrument is put forward as a thinking assessment instrument, can we trust it to consistently give us a thinking profile? If the instrument is promoted as an aptitude test, can we trust it to consistently give us a measure of aptitudes?

The second criterion for determining the quality of a psychometric instrument is its reliability. To be reliable, the instrument must produce consistent results on repeated administration. This should be particularly true of a personality, thinking, and aptitude instruments because, by definition, people are genetically predisposed to particular personality, thinking, and aptitude traits and it is thought that these traits become firmly established in early childhood and remain consistent over time. Therefore, a reliable assessment of the underlying traits should give consistent measurements over time. The following are reliability test results for the HBDI instrument.

Test-Retest Reliabilities for 78 Repeated Measures

Left	.96
Right	.96
A Quadrant	.86
B Quadrant	.93
C Quadrant	.94
D Quadrant	.97
Cerebral	.93
Limbic	.91
Intro/Extroversion	.73

Note. From "Improvement of Key Employee Retention Rates Through Attention to and Nurturance of Their Neuropsychological Preferences," by G. K. Bubenick, 2003, p. 23, doctoral dissertation, Northcentral University. Copyright 2003 by G. K. Bubenick. Retrieved June 22, 2005, from ProQuest Digital Dissertations database (AAT 3117956).

Table 1, Test - Retest Reliability

Psychological Profiling

Psychological profiling is the development of a theoretical description of an individual that may suggest that person's personality type, predisposition to ways of thinking and understanding, tendencies for types of behaviour, primary motivations, decision-making styles, etc. In the past, psychological profiling was commonly tied to criminal or aberrant behaviour, but now it's understood to be applicable to healthy individuals, as well. This type of information can aid the individual and others in understanding the things that will be challenging for them, and the things they may do with ease, enjoyment, and consistency. In addition, a psychological profile may be helpful in making a career path choice, and in resolving work-related and personal issues. Those situations and activities that a psychological profile reveals as easy for an individual might be referred to as their strengths. Those situations and activities that a psychological profile reveals as challenging for an individual might be referred to as their weaknesses. The more in-depth a psychological profile is, the more accurate it should be, and the more it will reveal about the individual. In this context, some personal coaches and business-training programs use multiple psychometric instruments in order to expand the individual profile.

Many different models for understanding an individual have been developed over the years to describe personality, thinking, behaviour, learning style, emotional intelligence, etc.

Typically, when research is undertaken, data are analyzed, and common elements are identified and grouped together into logical groupings. These groupings are defined, and the relationships between them is explained. Through this process, models are developed to summarize and explain the findings, to aid in understanding them, and to facilitate an exchange of ideas around them.

Models and Categorization

A theoretical model is a construct used to explain and add meaning to a theory. Within a theoretical model, there is often a classification scheme of some sort, where a large number of elements are grouped together into a manageable set of categories that conform to and illustrate aspects of the model. Theoretical models are typically used to explain and communicate the findings from empirical research that have been directed at discovering the natural laws governing a phenomenon. Theoretical models in psychology are also directed at functional goals, such as the need to understand and deal with social and business issues. The categorization scheme within a model provides a language for discussion and communication in addition to a framework for prediction, inference, and decision-making. When dealing with psychological models and categorization schemes, it is important to keep in mind that the models are human constructs used as aids in the communication, prediction, inference, and decision-making about the functioning of the mind as it relates to the particular issue of interest. It is important to keep in mind that theoretical psychological models are limited to the accuracy of the underlying theoretical model and the supporting research. Models should not be taken as absolute true renderings of what is actually happening in the brain. As psychological research continues, our understanding of the brain's workings increases and the models used to describe the phenomena continue to be revised and enhanced. Individuals' aptitudes, interests, talents, and other attributes exist across a continuum of human performance. They do not exist exclusively within a defined category in a particular model, nor are they limited to a specifically defined category. There is no inherent and universal truth in a model; they are structures of convenience. Some models are more easily communicated and understood than others, and their simplicity can be an advantage when introducing them to the general public or layperson. But a model's simplicity may also limit its usefulness in communication, prediction, inference, and decision-making about the functioning of the mind.

Some examples of psychological models and categorization schemes include Jung's psychological types, Maslow's hierarchy of needs, the American Psychiatric Association's Diagnostic and Statistical Manual of Mental Disorders, (DSM), the Myers-Briggs Type Indicator (MBTI), and the Big Five Personality Trait Theory.

The Psychometric Proposition

There was a recent article published in Yahoo News dealing with the question of whether personality tests (specifically the MBTI) should be used in hiring.

The MBTI is a personality instrument (within one definition of personality) that has been validated for that purpose. However, there is much more to human performance than personality, and it should be kept in mind that personality is a human construct and is not immutable.

By now, the reader should understand that neurological research has gone beyond the dark ages, and that our understanding of the brain and brain function is considerably more advanced than it was even ten years ago. Who we are happens in the brain, and the brain is completely constrained within biological processes. The processes work consistently, and each individual has their own limitations within them. What gives us pleasure is consistent, and what causes us pain is consistent. How we perform is constrained by our physiological limits, including the physiological limits of the brain. How we perform is determined by more than our personality: consider athletic, academic, leisure, and, yes, job performance. Factors that may be more indicative of our potential job performance might be identified as talents, interests, attitudes, and experience.

Psychometrics is closely tied to our understanding of the brain, as well as to our greater understanding of the complete individual.

More and more, this understanding is being quantified. Along with the advances in research, there is an ever-growing body of psychometric instruments being developed and refined, and the argument for including psychometric assessments in the job environment and larger business world is getting stronger.

Concepts In Psychology That Are Relevant To Business

Intelligence

Intelligence has been defined as a very general mental capability that, among other things, involves the ability to reason, plan, solve problems, think abstractly, comprehend complex ideas, learn quickly, and learn from experience. Intelligence is not only book learning, a narrow academic skill, or the ability to respond to different types of mentally challenging tests. Rather, intelligence reflects a broader and deeper capability for comprehending our surroundings—"catching on," "making sense" of things, and "figuring out" what to do. (http://en.wikipedia.org/wiki/Intelligence)

In an attempt to expand on the above definition, the Board of Scientific Affairs of the American Psychological Association offers the following comment ("Intelligence: Knowns and Unknowns," Board of Scientific Affairs of the American Psychological Association, 1995):

> "Individuals differ from one another in their ability to understand complex ideas, to adapt effectively to the environment, to learn from experience, to engage in various forms of reasoning, to overcome obstacles by taking thought. Although these individual differences can be substantial, they are never entirely consistent: a given person's intellectual performance will vary on different

occasions, in different domains, as judged by different criteria. Concepts of "intelligence" are attempts to clarify and organize this complex set of phenomena. Although considerable clarity has been achieved in some areas, no such conceptualization has yet answered all the important questions, and none commands universal assent. Indeed, when two dozen prominent theorists were recently asked to define intelligence, they gave two dozen, somewhat different, definitions."

The concept of intelligence may be further broken down into the concepts of fluid and crystalized intelligence.

Fluid intelligence is the ability to think and reason abstractly, effectively solve problems, and think strategically. It is more commonly known as "street smarts," or the ability to "quickly think on your feet." Fluid intelligence can be very important in types of work that require quick decision-making in unstructured situations, such as in-the-moment competitive situations.

Crystallized intelligence is the ability to learn from past experiences, and to apply this learning to work-related situations. Work situations that require crystallized intelligence include those that require producing and analyzing written reports, comprehending work instructions, using numbers as tools to make effective decisions, etc.

Most IQ tests attempt to measure both types of intelligence.
(5/11/2015, https://en.wikipedia.org/wiki/Fluid_and_crystallized_intelligence)

Aptitude

An aptitude is a component of a person's competency to do a certain kind of work at a certain level, which can also be considered a «talent." Aptitudes may be physical or mental. An aptitude is not knowledge, understanding, learned or acquired abilities (skills), or attitude. The innate nature of aptitude is in contrast to achievement, which represents knowledge or ability that is gained.

Aptitude and intelligence quotient (IQ) are not the same thing, however aptitude and IQ are related—and in some ways, opposite—views of human mental ability. Whereas IQ sees intelligence as a single, measurable characteristic affecting all mental ability, aptitude refers to one of many different characteristics that can be independent of each other, such as aptitude for military flight, air traffic control, computer programming, music, dance, etc.. This view of aptitude is supportive of the theory of multiple intelligences.

An important consideration when trying to anticipate job performance based on the results of an aptitude tests is that IQ differences can make the differences in the results on aptitude tests insignificant. The performance of an individual with a high aptitude and lower intelligence may be equaled by the performance of an individual with a less aptitude and higher intelligence. The converse may also be true: a person of high aptitude and lower intelligence may also rival the performance of an individual of high intelligence and less aptitude.

It has been shown that individuals in similar occupations tend to achieve similar results on aptitude tests. The critical significance of aptitude may be as an indicator of whether an individual will be inclined to continue performing well.

Combined Aptitude and Knowledge Assessments

Some assessment instruments evaluate both aptitude and intelligence. An example is the Armed Services Vocational Aptitude Battery (ASVAB), given to recruits entering the armed forces of the United States. Another example is the SAT, which is designed as a test of aptitude for college admission in the United States, but also features achievement elements. For example, the SAT tests mathematical reasoning, which depends on both innate mathematical ability and mathematics education.

Skills

(http://en.wikipedia.org/wiki/Skill)

A skill is defined as the learned ability to carry out a task with pre-determined results, often within a given amount of time, energy, or both. Skills can often be divided into domain-general and domain-specific. For example, in the domain of work, some general skills include time management, teamwork, leadership, and self-motivation, whereas domain-specific skills are useful only for a certain job.

A better concept of skill may be gained by considering the following sixteen basic skills deemed essential to achieving optimum performance in today's work environment:

1. Foundation Skill: learning how to learn
2. Reading Competence
3. Writing Competence
4. Computation (mathematics) competence
5. Communication: listening (interpersonal skill)
6. Communication: oral (verbalize thoughts, interpersonal skills)
7. Adaptability: creative thinking (and conceptualization)
8. Adaptability: problem-solving (and organization)
9. Personal Management: self-esteem and self-care
10. Personal Management: goal-setting/motivation

11. Personal Management: personal/career development
12. Group Effectiveness: interpersonal skills
13. Group Effectiveness: negotiation (resolve conflict)
14. Group Effectiveness: teamwork
15. Influence: organizational effectiveness
16. Influence: leadership (and shared leadership)

Emotional Intelligence

Emotional Intelligence (EQ) is a relatively recent behavioural model that rose to prominence with Daniel Goleman's 1995 book, *Emotional Intelligence*. Emotional intelligence theory was originally developed during the 1970s and 1980s, and was promoted in the work and writings of psychologists Howard Gardner (Harvard), Peter Salovey (Yale), and John "Jack" Mayer (New Hampshire). Underlying the development of EQ has been the basic premise that being a successful leader requires an effective awareness, control, and management of one's own emotions, and those of other people.

Emotional intelligence has been defined as an individual's ability to identify and manage their own emotions and the emotions of others. It is generally said to include three skills:

1. Emotional awareness, including an individual's ability to identify their emotions and those of others.

2. The ability to harness emotions and apply them to tasks like thinking and problem-solving.

3. The ability to manage emotions, including your own, and to cheer up or calm down other people.

(http://www.psychologytoday.com/basics/emotional-intelligence)

Emotional intelligence has also been defined as the capacity to reason about emotions and emotional information, and to have emotions enhance thought. People with high EQs are thought to be able to solve a variety of emotion-related problems accurately and quickly. (http://www.psychologytoday.com/blog/the-personality-analyst/200909/what-emotional-intelligence-is-and-is-not)

Going beyond the definitions, there are currently three models for emotional intelligence: ability-based, trait-based, and mixed.

Ability Model

The ability-based model views emotions as useful sources of information that help us make sense of and navigate the social environment. It proposes that individuals vary in their ability to process information of an emotional nature and to relate emotional processing to a wider cognition. This ability is seen to manifest itself in certain adaptive behaviours. The ability model claims that EQ includes four types of abilities.

Perceiving emotions is the ability to detect and decipher emotions in faces, pictures, voices, and cultural artifacts, and also in oneself. Perceiving emotions represents a basic aspect of emotional intelligence, as it makes all other processing of emotional information possible.

Using emotions is the ability to harness emotions to facilitate various cognitive activities such as thinking and problem solving. The emotionally intelligent person can capitalize fully on their changing moods in order to best fit the task at hand.

Understanding emotions is the ability to comprehend the language of emotion and to appreciate complicated relationships among emotions. For example, understanding emotions encompasses the ability to be sensitive to slight variations between emotions, and to recognize and describe how emotions evolve over time.

Managing emotions is the ability to regulate emotions in both ourselves and in others. Therefore, the emotionally intelligent person

can harness emotions, even negative ones, and manage them to achieve intended goals.
(http://en.wikipedia.org/wiki/Emotional_intelligence)

Trait Model

Trait EQ is viewed as "a constellation of emotional self-perceptions located at the lower levels of personality." In lay terms, trait EQ refers to an individual's self-perceptions of their emotional abilities. This model of EQ encompasses behavioural dispositions and self-perceived abilities and is measured by self-report, as opposed to the ability-based model, which refers to actual abilities. Trait EQ should be investigated within a personality framework. An alternative label for the same construct is "trait emotional self-efficacy."

Mixed Model

The mixed model focuses on EQ as a wide array of competencies and skills that drive leadership performance. Goleman's model outlines five main EQ constructs and as referenced in Wikipedia "(for more details see "What Makes A Leader" by Daniel Goleman, best of *Harvard Business Review* 1998)(http://en.wikipedia.org/wiki/Emotional_intelligence).

Self-awareness is the ability to know one's emotions, strengths, weaknesses, drives, values, and goals, and to recognize their impact on others while using gut feelings to guide decisions.

Self-regulation involves controlling or redirecting one's disruptive emotions and impulses and adapting to changing circumstances.

Social skill is managing relationships to move people in a desired direction.

Empathy is considering other people's feelings, especially when making decisions.

Motivation is being driven to achieve for the sake of achievement.

(http://en.wikipedia.org/wiki/Emotional_intelligence)

Intelligence and emotional intelligence are quite different concepts, and both may be considered aspects of personality. If a psychological profiler wanted to broaden the profile on an individual, and wanted to take into consideration all three aspects—personality, intelligence, and emotional intelligence—and wished to use psychometric instruments to standardize the assessment, then the profiler would need to use three different instruments: a specialized instrument for each aspect being assessed.

Emotional intelligence is proving increasingly relevant to organizational and individual development, because EQ principles provide a new way to understand and assess people's behaviours, management styles, attitudes, interpersonal skills, and potential. Emotional intelligence is proving to be an important consideration in human-resources planning, job profiling, recruitment interviewing and selection, management development, customer relations and customer service, and more (http://www.businessballs.com/eq.htm).

An example of an EQ assessment instrument is the Mayer-Salovey-Caruso Emotional Intelligence Test (MSCEIT). This assessment instrument is an ability-based test designed to measure the four branches of the EI model of Mayer and Salovey.

The four branches of emotional intelligence included in this instrument are:

1. **Perceiving emotions**: The ability to perceive emotions in oneself and others as well as in objects, art, stories, music, and other stimuli.

2. **Facilitating thought**: The ability to generate, use, and feel emotion as necessary to communicate feelings or employ them in other cognitive processes.

3. **Understanding emotions**: The ability to understand emotional information, to understand how emotions combine and progress through relationship transitions, and to appreciate such emotional meanings.

4. **Managing emotions**: The ability to be open to feelings, and to modulate them in oneself and others so as to promote personal understanding and growth.

As MSCEIT is an ability-based test, which means that you can get a low score on it, but, through hard work and effort, can behave in an emotionally intelligent manner. Conversely, you could get a high score on the MSCEIT but not utilize the emotional abilities that you possess (http://www.bestpracticeconsulting.com.au/team-building/self-awareness-tools, 2016-02-21).

Personality Theories

Personality may be the most popular psychological construct in the mind of the layperson. The term personality is used freely in everyday language to refer to many aspects of human nature. The Oxford dictionary defines personality as the combination of characteristics or qualities that form an individual's distinctive character (http://www.oxforddictionaries.com/definition/english/personality). About.com defines personality as the characteristic patterns of thoughts, feelings, and behaviours that make a person unique. In addition, about.com states, "personality arises from within the individual and remains fairly consistent throughout life" (http://psychology.about.com/od/overviewofpersonality/a/persondef.htm, 14-Mar-16). Another perspective, by the American Psychological Association, focuses on differences: "personality refers to individual differences in characteristic patterns of thinking, feeling, and behaving" (http://www.apa.org/topics/personality/, 14-Mar-16). Basically, we are recognized through our personalities as unique individuals, and our personalities tend to be consistent over time.
(5/10/2015, http://www.oxforddictionaries.com/definition/english/personality).

However, there are authors who would include in this definition of personality the environmental effects an individual experiences during early childhood development. One way of conceptualizing personality is to consider the characteristic elements an individual would display while playing at an early age (five, six, or seven years old). If you were to meet that playmate again at a later age (say while in her forties, fifties, or sixties), you would still recognize them as the same person you had played with so many years ago. Those identifying characteristic elements are likely to be personality traits. It is these aspects of characteristic traits and stability over time that are relevant in the identifying personality.

According to Wikipedia, different personality theorists present their own definitions of the personality based on their theoretical positions—and there are many theories of personality. This text will present the 16-Personality-Factor Theory, the Big Five Personality Trait Theory, Enneagram, True Colors, and Psychological Types.

16-Personality-Factor Theory

The 16-Personality-Factor Theory (16PF Theory) was identified in 1946 by Raymond Cattell. Cattell used the emerging technology of computers to analyze a list of 4,500 adjectives through the statistical technique of factor analysis. This process allowed the use of ratings by observation, questionnaires, and objective measurements of actual behaviour. Initially, there were twelve acknowledged and four covert factors identified that made up the original sixteen primary personality factors. Following on the 16PF Theory, a five-factor theory was proposed by Ernest Tupes and Raymond Christal in 1961 (https://en.wikipedia.org/wiki/Big_Five_personality_traits), gained acceptance. At the same time, research continued on the 16PF Theory, and subsequent analysis resulted in the identification of five factors underlying the sixteen factors. Cattell called these five factors "global factors."

Relationship to Five Factor Models

In the fourth (1967) and fifth (1993) editions of the 16PF Theory, it was acknowledged that the five global factors seemed to correspond fairly closely to the "big five personality traits." In fact, the development of the "big-five" factors began by factor-analyzing the original items of the 16PF. In 1963, W. T. Norman replicated Cattell's work and suggested that five factors would be sufficient.

http://en.wikipedia.org/wiki/16_Personality_Factors

Big Five Personality Trait Theory

The Big Five Personality Trait Theory is one of the more prominent personality models in contemporary psychology. This theory incorporates five different variables into a conceptual model for describing personality.

In the development of this model, it became evident to many psychologists that five factors were sufficient for describing personality; it was also recognized that there needed to be clear definition as to what those five factors were. In 1998, through extensive debate and experimentation, general consensus arose around the identity of the five factors and their basic interpretation. These five different factors are often referred to as the Big Five.

The Big Five Personality Trait Theory is among the newest models developed for the description of personality. It shows promise and is considered among the most practical and applicable models available in the field of personality psychology.

The five factors are
(https://en.wikipedia.org/wiki/Big_Five_personality_traits):

1. **Openness** (inventive/curious vs. consistent/cautious). Openness reflects a person's degree of intellectual curiosity, creativity, and preference for novelty and variety. It is also described as the extent to which a person is imaginative or independent and depicts a personal preference for a variety of activities over a strict routine. High openness can be perceived as unpredictability or lack of focus. Moreover, individuals

with high openness are said to pursue self-actualization specifically by seeking out intense, euphoric experiences, such as skydiving, living abroad, and gambling. Conversely, those with low openness seek to gain fulfillment through perseverance and are characterized as pragmatic and data-driven—sometimes even dogmatic and close-minded. Some disagreement remains about how to interpret and contextualize the openness factor.

2. **Conscientiousness** (efficient/organized vs. easy-going/careless). A tendency to be organized and dependable, show self-discipline, act dutifully, aim for achievement, and prefer planned rather than spontaneous behaviour. Individuals displaying high conscientiousness are often perceived as stubborn and obsessive, while individuals displaying low conscientiousness are typically seen as flexible and spontaneous, but they can also be perceived as sloppy and unreliable.

3. **Extroversion** (outgoing/energetic vs. solitary/reserved). A tendency to display energy, positive emotions, urgency, assertiveness, and sociability. Also, a tendency to seek stimulation in the company of others, and talkativeness. High extroversion is often perceived as attention-seeking and domineering. Low extroversion produces a reserved, reflective personality, which can be perceived as aloof or self-absorbed.

4. **Agreeableness**:(friendly/compassionate vs. analytical/detached). A tendency to be compassionate and cooperative rather than suspicious and antagonistic toward others. It is also a measure of one's trusting and helpful nature, and whether a person is generally well-tempered or not. High agreeableness is often seen as naive or submissive. Low agreeableness personalities are often competitive or challenging people, traits that can be seen as argumentative or untrustworthy.

5. **Neuroticism** (sensitive/nervous vs. secure/confident). A tendency to experience unpleasant emotions easily, such as anger, anxiety, depression, and vulnerability. Neuroticism also considers someone's degree of emotional stability and impulse control and is sometimes referred to by its low pole, "emotional stability." A high need for stability manifests as a stable and calm personality, but this can be seen as uninspiring and unconcerned. A low need for stability causes a reactive and excitable personality; these are often very dynamic individuals, but they can be perceived as unstable or insecure.

Enneagram

(https://www.enneagraminstitute.com/)

Don Riso proposed the Enneagram Theory in 1977; subsequent development on the theory was performed by Russ Hudson.

The Enneagram Theory proposes nine personality types and nine levels of development for a framework for understanding an individual's personality. In addition, there is the concept of "wing." A person's personality type usually includes the person's basic type along with the one or two types adjacent to it on the circumference of the Enneagram—the "wing." (See more at: https://www.enneagraminstitute.com/how-the-enneagram-system-works/#sthash.4X4aNpru.dpuf.)

According to Enneagram theory, in order to understand an individual accurately, it is necessary to perceive where they lie along the continuum of levels of their type at a given time. In other words, one must assess whether a person is in their healthy, average, or unhealthy range of functioning. This is important because two people of the same personality type and wing will differ significantly if one is healthy and the other unhealthy. In relationships and the business world, an appreciation for this distinction is crucial.

In general, the personality types presented in the Enneagram are as follows:

1. **Reformer.** Reformers are conscientious and ethical, with a strong sense of right and wrong. They are teachers, crusaders, and advocates for change. They are always striving to improve things, but afraid of making a mistake. Well-organized, orderly, and fastidious, they try to maintain high standards, but can slip into being critical and perfectionistic. They typically have problems with resentment and impatience. At their best, they are wise, discerning, realistic, and noble. They can be morally heroic. See more at: https://www.enneagraminstitute.com/type-1/#sthash.jISHArlJ.dpuf.

2. **Helper.** Helpers are empathetic, sincere, and warm-hearted. They are friendly, generous, and self-sacrificing, but they can also be sentimental, flattering, and people-pleasing. They are well-meaning and driven to be close to others, but can slip into doing things for others in order to be needed. They typically have problems with possessiveness and acknowledging their own needs. At their best, they are unselfish and altruistic, and have unconditional love for others. See more at: https://www.enneagraminstitute.com/type-2/#sthash.XjDfupGF.dpuf.

3. **Achiever.** Achievers are self-assured, attractive, and charming. Ambitious, competent, and energetic, they can also be status-conscious and highly driven for advancement. They are diplomatic and poised but can also be overly concerned with their image and what others think of them. They typically have problems with workaholism and competitiveness. At their best, they are self-accepting, authentic, and everything they seem to be—role models who inspire others. See more at: https://www.enneagraminstitute.com/type-3/#sthash.FUGZhSVP.dpuf.

4. **Individualist**. Individualists are self-aware, sensitive, and reserved. They are emotionally honest, creative, and personal, but can also be moody and self-conscious. They tend to withhold themselves from others due to feeling vulnerable and defective, and they can also feel disdainful and exempt from ordinary ways of living. They typically have problems with melancholy, self-indulgence, and self-pity. At their best they are inspired and highly creative; they are able to renew themselves and transform their experiences. See more at: https://www.enneagraminstitute.com/type-4/#sthash.eI9DNnvj.dpuf.

5. **Investigator**. Investigators are alert, insightful, and curious. They are able to concentrate and focus on developing complex ideas and skills. Independent, innovative, and inventive, they can also become preoccupied with their thoughts and imaginary constructs. They become detached, yet high-strung and intense. They typically have problems with eccentricity, nihilism, and isolation. At their best they are visionary pioneers, often ahead of their time, and are able to see the world in an entirely new way. See more at: https://www.enneagraminstitute.com/type-5/#sthash.KteUG2oM.dpuf.

6. **Loyalist**. Loyalists are committed, security-oriented types. Loyalists are reliable, hard-working, responsible, and trustworthy. Excellent "troubleshooters," they foresee problems and foster cooperation, but can also become defensive, evasive, and anxious; they run on stress while complaining about it. They can be cautious and indecisive, but also reactive, defiant, and rebellious. They typically have problems with self-doubt and suspicion. At their best, they are internally stable and self-reliant, courageously championing themselves and others. See more at: https://www.enneagraminstitute.com/type-6/#sthash.oeCbGzve.dpuf.

7. **Enthusiast**. Enthusiasts are extroverted, optimistic, versatile, and spontaneous. Playful, high-spirited, and practical, they can also misapply their many talents, becoming overextended, scattered, and undisciplined. They constantly seek new and exciting experiences but can become distracted and exhausted by staying on the go. They typically have problems with impatience and impulsiveness. At their best, they focus their talents on worthwhile goals, becoming appreciative, joyous, and satisfied. See more at: https://www.enneagraminstitute.com/type-7/#sthash.7OqgTBCr.dpuf

8. **Challenger**. Challengers are self-confident, strong, and assertive. Protective, resourceful, straight-talking, and decisive, they may also be egocentric and domineering. Challengers feel they must control their environment, especially people, sometimes becoming confrontational and intimidating. Challengers typically have problems with their tempers and with allowing themselves to be vulnerable. At their best, they are self-mastering and use their strength to improve others' lives, becoming heroic, magnanimous, and inspiring. See more at: https://www.enneagraminstitute.com/type-8/#sthash.rl12CS96.dpuf.

9. **Peacemaker**. Peacemakers are accepting, trusting, and stable. They are usually creative, optimistic, and supportive, but can also be too willing to go along with others to keep the peace. They want everything to go smoothly and be without conflict, but they can also tend to be complacent, simplifying problems and minimizing anything upsetting. They typically have problems with inertia and stubbornness. At their best, they are indomitable and all-embracing, and they are able to bring people together and heal conflicts. See more at: https://www.enneagraminstitute.com/type-9/#sthash.nzUP195y.dpuf.

See more at: https://www.enneagraminstitute.com/how-the-enneagram-system-works/#sthash.6U5r1zke.dpuf.

True Colors

The theory behind True Colors can be traced back to when Hippocrates, 460 BC, identified the four different temperaments of humans—sanguine, choleric, phlegmatic, and melancholic—and to Plato's ideas about character and personality in 428 BC.

The True Colors instrument today

In 1978, Don Lowry formed True Colors International, and introduced the True Colors instrument, which uses colour to represent four general personality types. Theoretically, True Colors is based on the Keirsey Temperament Sorter, which is an adaptation of the Myers-Briggs Type Indicator (MBTI) (Cooper, 2009, p. 3). The colours and traits associated with the colour are as follows:

ORANGE: Witty, charming, spontaneous, impulsive, generous, impactful, optimistic, eager, bold, physical, immediate, fraternal.

GOLD: Loyal, dependable, prepared, thorough, sensible, punctual, faithful, stable, organized, caring, concerned, concrete.

GREEN: Analytical, global, conceptual, cool, calm, collected, inventive, logical, perfectionistic, abstract, hypothetical, investigative.

BLUE: Enthusiastic, sympathetic, personal, warm, communicative, compassionate, idealistic, spiritual, sincere, peaceful, flexible, imaginative.

True Colors uses colour to distill elaborate concepts of personality theory into a user-friendly, easy-to-understand, easy-to-remember, and easy-to-apply tool that is employed to foster healthy, productive relationships among co-workers, friends, and family.

Personality, Thinking, and Behaviour: MBTI, HBDI, and DISC
Myers-Briggs Type Indicator

(http://www.myersbriggs.org/my-mbti-personality-type/mbti-basics/)

The Myers-Briggs Type Indicator (MBTI) was developed by Catherine C. Briggs and her daughter, Isabel Briggs Myers, based on the work of Swiss psychiatrist Carl Jung, who presented his psychological-type theory in his book on psychological types, published in 1921 and translated to English in 1923. Jung believed that our preferences do not change; they stay the same over time, which is a basic tenet of personality theory.

The MBTI model consists of four pairs of opposites. Like our right and left hands, we can use either hand, but mostly favour a preference for one over the other. The MBTI is used to determine which of the dichotomies the individual is likely presenting.

The MBTI instrument is a type indicator, not a test. It is a forced-choice questionnaire that looks only at normal behaviour. There are no right or wrong answers; a person should answer as they see fit and be true to themselves. There are no good types or bad types. All types have some natural strengths and some natural deficiencies (weaknesses). The MBTI provides practical results that can be used in self-discovery, team development, communication, decision-making, and problem-solving.

The MBTI theory proposes four dichotomies with foci on energy, judgment, perception, and orientation. The dichotomies associated with each focus are as follows:

Energy: Introversion (I) and Extroversion (E)

Judgment: Thinking (T) and Feeling (F)
Perception: Sensing (S) and Intuition (N)
Orientation: Judging (J) and Perceiving (P)

The combination of these elements means there are sixteen personality types that can be presented as follows:

ISTJ	ISFJ	INFJ	INTJ
Responsible Executors	Dedicated Stewards	Insightful Motivators	Visionary Strategists
ISTP	**ISFP**	**INFP**	**INTP**
Nimble Pragmatics	Practical Custodians	Inspired Crusaders	Expansive Analyzers
ESTP	**ESFP**	**ENFP**	**ENTP**
Dynamic Mavericks	Enthusiastic Improvisors	Impassioned Catalysts	Innovative Explorers
ESTJ	**ESFJ**	**ENFJ**	**ENTJ**
Efficient Drivers	Committed Builders	Engaging Mobilizers	Strategic Directors

Table 2, MBTI Model

The foregoing discussion of personality theories and instruments amounts to nowhere near a comprehensive inventory. The objective here has been to introduce the reader to some popular personality theories that have some traction in the business environment. With this information, it is hoped that the reader will conduct their own investigation into personality instruments, and, if appropriate, choose the one that's most conducive to their specific needs.

Personality

Studies have been done to investigate the correspondence between the various personality theories. The studies done in the following relationships are reported in Wikipedia (https://en.wikipedia.org/wiki/Myers%E2%80%93Briggs_Type_Indicator#Keirsey_temperaments):

IS_IT_EJ	IS_IF_EJ	IN_IF_EJ	IN_IT_EJ
Inspector	Protector	Counselor	Mastermind
IS_ET_IP	IS_EF_IP	IN_EF_IP	IN_ET_IP
Crafter	Composer	Healer	Architect
ES_ET_IP	ES_EF_IP	EN_EF_IP	EN_ET_IP
Promoter	Performer	Champion	Inventor
ES_IT_EJ	ES_IF_EJ	EN_IF_EJ	EN_IT_EJ
Supervisor	Provider	Teacher	Fieldmarshal

Table 3, Keirsey and MBTI

3

As indicated above, David W. Keirsey was able to map four "temperaments" to the existing Myers–Briggs system groupings: SP, SJ, NF, and NT. Though it is reflective of some commonality, the Keirsey Temperament Sorter is not considered to be directly associated with the official MBTI.

	Extraversion	Openness	Agreeableness	Conscientiousness	Neuroticism
E-I	**−0.74**	0.03	−0.03	0.08	0.16
S-N	0.10	**0.72**	0.04	−0.15	−0.06
T-F	0.19	0.02	**0.44**	−0.15	0.06
J-P	0.15	0.30	−0.06	**−0.49**	0.11

The closer the number is to 1.0 or −1.0, the higher the degree of correlation.

Table 4, Big Five and MBTI

Table 4 presents the results of a correlational analysis performed by McCrae and Costa. This analysis found that the four MBTI indices did measure aspects of four of the five major dimensions of normal personality.

The results of these types of studies indicate that, although there may not yet be absolute agreement on what constitutes personality, there is some consistency in the theories and models being pursued.

Thinking

Thinking is defined as the action of using your mind to produce ideas, decisions, memories, etc.; "thinking" is the biological brain activity of considering something (http://www.merriam-webster.com/dictionary/thinking). In the realm of psychometric instruments that assess thinking preferences, the field is limited; one of the more popular instruments is the Herrmann Brain Dominance Instrument (HBDI). It is a very popular choice for research that requires information with respect to thinking profiles.

Herrmann Brain Dominance Instrument

The model for the HBDI comes from two different theoretical sources. The first is the triune brain. as proposed by Paul MacLean (1960s, https://en.wikipedia.org/wiki/Triune_brain); the second is the split-brain theory, proposed by Roger Sperry (1967, https://en.wikipedia.org/wiki/Split-brain). Ned Herrmann brought the two brain theories together and proposed a model containing four quadrants. He performed psychological testing to validate the model. His model is not intended to be a map of the brain but, rather, a model that presents conceptual aspects of thinking that facilitate understanding of the individual based on thinking preferences.

Sidebar: Alan Alda clip on the split brain (http://www.youtube.com/watch?v=82tlVcq6E7A).

Split-brain research suggests that if the physiological structure to support a brain function does not exist, neither will the function. Similarly, it suggests that for a mental activity to exist, there must be a supporting brain structure.

The Whole Brain Model

Ned Herrmann's whole brain model consists of four quadrants labelled, tagged with letters, and colour-coded for ease of learning, retention, and discussion.

The Rational Self (A-Quadrant, Blue)

> The Rational Quadrant is characterized as representing logical, analytical, challenging, critical, definitive, direct, factual, intellectual, and quantitative characteristics. Individuals expressing this quadrant are typically seen as unemotional, unable to relate, uncompromising, overly focused, limited in their creativity, systems-focused, uncomfortable with ambiguity, and suffering from paralysis of analysis.

The Safekeeping Self (B-Quadrant, Green)

> The Safekeeping Quadrant presents characteristics such as administrative, articulate, controlled, detailed, disciplined, dominant, industrious, organized, persistent, planning, practical, procedural, punctual, safekeeping, sequential, and structured. Individuals expressing this quadrant may also be viewed as controlling, rigid, myopic, unimaginative, resistant to change, uptight, and stubborn.

The Feelings Self (C-Quadrant, Red)

> The Feelings Quadrant presents characteristics such as interpersonal, cooperative, emotional, empathic, enthusiastic, expressive, friendly, harmonious, kinesthetic, and helpful. Individuals expressing this quadrant may also be viewed as overly sensitive, overly emotional,

not time-efficient, not fact-based, irrational, imprecise, and tending to have difficulty making decisions.

The Experimental Self (D-Quadrant, Yellow)

The Experimental Quadrant presents characteristics such as holistic, adventurous, artistic, conceptual, creative, curious, exploratory, flexible, intuitive, integrating, and synthesizing. Individuals expressing this quadrant may also be viewed as flaky, distracted, unrealistic, not fact-based, absent-minded, unfocused, and resistant to structure and authority. They may be accused of trying to reinvent the wheel.

Personality and Thinking

There has been research conducted to determine if there is a relationship between the concepts of personality types and thinking preferences. (Bunderson, 1985), (DeWald, 1989) As a result of the work performed by Bunderson, the following relationship might be depicted:

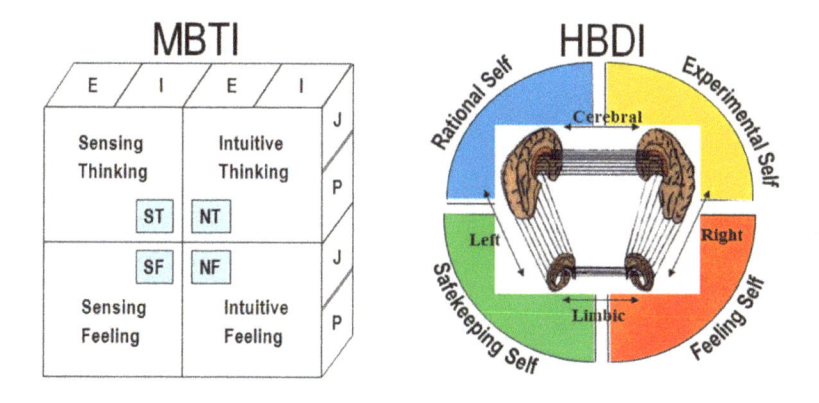

Image 27, MBTI and HBDI

Image 27 indicates a possible correspondence between the MBTI and the HBDI. The diagram suggests there may be correspondences between the sensing and thinking elements of the MBTI and the rational self of the HBDI, the intuitive and thinking elements of the MBTI and the experimental self of the HBDI, the sensing and feeling elements of the MBTI and the safekeeping self of the HBDI, and the intuitive and feeling elements of the MBTI and the feeling self of the HBDI. In fact, in MBTI literature, the judgment (thinking/feeling) and perception (sensing/intuition) dichotomies are often referred to as the "Thinking Dichotomies or Quadrants."

Behaviour

According (in part) to Wikipedia, behaviour is the response of a system or organism to various stimuli or inputs, whether internal or external, conscious or subconscious, overt or covert, voluntary or involuntary. From a biological perspective, behaviours can be either innate or learned. Behaviour is believed to be influenced by the endocrine system and the nervous system; it is commonly believed that the complexity of an organism's behaviour is correlated with the complexity of its nervous system (https://en.wikipedia.org/wiki/Behaviour).

It should be recognized that a key aspect of behaviour (in contrast to personality and thinking) is that behaviour is changeable. An entity may change its behaviour in response to external or internal stimuli—but even when the behaviour has changed, the entity's personality will remain consistent. In terms of thinking, an entity may change its thinking "behaviour" at will, but the entity's thinking *preferences* will remain consistent.

Behaviour Assessment Tools

Much of behaviour assessment has been focused on abnormal and aberrant behaviour. In the context of assessment instruments that are specific to behaviour and appropriate for business use, one of the more popular tools is the DISC instrument. Indeed, DISC has grown to become possibly the most widely used behavioural assessment tool in the world (https://www.axiomsoftware.com/disc/history-and-development-of-disc-hippocrates-jung-marston.php).

DISC

The DISC is a behaviour-assessment tool based on the DISC theory proposed by psychologist William Moulton Marston in his book *Emotions of Normal People,* published in 1928. It was not until 1956 when Walter Clarke, an industrial psychologist, developed the DISC theory into a behaviour-assessment instrument.

DISC theory proposes that behaviour types can be inferred from an individual's sense of self and interaction with the environment. Marston proposed the use of two indices: the environment, and the individual's sense of their ability to respond to (or control) their environment. The environmental index is depicted as being unfavourable at one end and favourable at the other. For illustrative purposes, an unfavourable view of the environment would be like a person going to a party and having a frame of mind that it won't necessarily be a good party, or that the food there won't be very good, whereas a person who views the environment as favourable would be of a frame of mind that it's going to be a great party, or that the food there is going to be great. The control index is depicted as being "unable to control" at one end and "able to control" at the other. To illustrate this concept, consider again the party scenario. The individual who holds the viewpoint that they are not able to control the environment would have the mindset that "it might be a good party, or it might be a lousy party—either way, there's not much I can do about it." The person who feels they are able to control the environment would approach the scenario with the mindset: "It's a party, and I'm going to have a great time." The two indices were super-imposed on top of each other, resulting in a quadrant construct. Marston added the labels for the quadrants as Dominance (D), Influence (I), Steadiness (S), and Compliance (C). Assembling the first letter of each of the quadrant labels resulted in the DISC title.

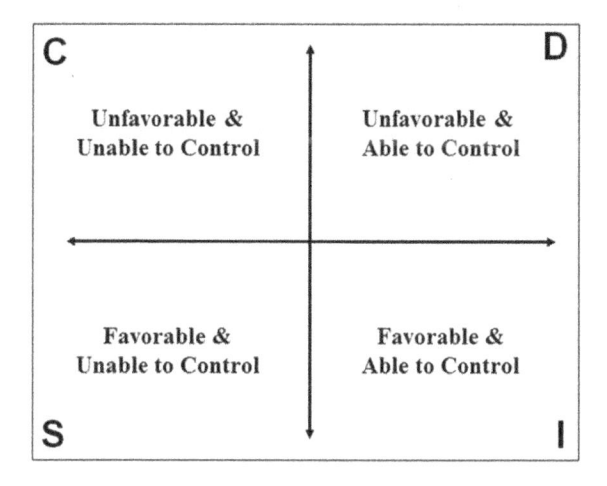

```
       C ↑                    D
   Unfavorable &         Unfavorable &
   Unable to Control     Able to Control

←─────────────────────────────────────→

   Favorable &           Favorable &
   Unable to Control     Able to Control

       S     ↓                I
```

Image 28, DISC Theoretical Model

The "D" style (Dominance) is described as aggressive, competitive, demanding, in a hurry. They interrupt others, are direct, like to challenge people, are starters (not finishers), tend to see things as white or black (not grey), like being in control, exceed authority, get bored easily, and aren't fond of listening. The primary fear for the "D"-style personality is loss of control.

The "I" style (Influencer) is described as tending to be talkative, social, impulsive, communicative, very excitable, and quick to agree. They will tolerate a small personal space, they promise more than they can deliver, they are always selling but avoid details, they don't like boring and strict people, they forget rules, they are prone to frequently making small mistakes, and they are good with people. The primary fear for the "I"-style personality is social rejection.

The "S" style (Steady) is described as tending to be thorough, steady, systematic, polite, modest, and secure in a stable environment. They tend to proceed with caution, they are down to earth, stay in the background, and listen more than they talk. They tend to need instruction, they resist sudden change, they have strong principles, they either like or dislike people, they tend to be team oriented, and reliable. The primary fear for the "S"-style personality is loss of stability.

The "C" style (Compliance) is described as tending to be exact, perfectionistic, logical, and analytical. These folks have a fear of being wrong, they tend to obey the law and rules, and they look for order. They can be quiet and matter-of-fact, despite inspiration; however, they may not be very inspiring They tend to be detail- and rule-oriented and risk averse, and they can be diplomatically polite. The primary fear for the "C" behaviour style is criticism of their work.

An interesting aspect of the DISC instrument is that the DISC theory exists in the public domain, which means there are many slightly different renditions of the tool and some discordant advancements or inclusions. Some providers of a DISC-type instrument try to pass it off as a personality-assessment tool. This is misleading. As discussed above, behaviour is not the same as personality, and the DISC has been developed and validated as a behavior-assessment tool. To promote it otherwise is not right.

Thinking and Behaviour

A comparison of HBDI and Extended DISC

In 2007, the author (Wilson, 2007) performed a comparative analysis of the HBDI and Extended DISC tools (one of the proprietary tools based on the DISC theory) as part of a PhD dissertation. The research indicated that the tools were viewed as being distinctly different and that they assess different aspects (thinking and behaviour) of humans. The results of this research, indicated the possibility of the following relationships:

From the HBDI perspective:

- "Rational" (A quadrant) individuals tend to view the environment as unfavourable.

- "Left-brain" individuals tend to have a view that they are unable to control their environment.

- "Right-brain" individuals tend to have the view that they can control their environment.

- "Feelings"-type (C quadrant) individuals tend to view the environment as favourable.

- From an Extended DISC perspective:

- "Cerebral" individuals tend to view the environment as unfavourable.

- "Compliance" individuals tend to be left-brained.

- "Influencer" individuals tend to be right-brained.

- "Limbic" individuals tend to view the environment as favourable.

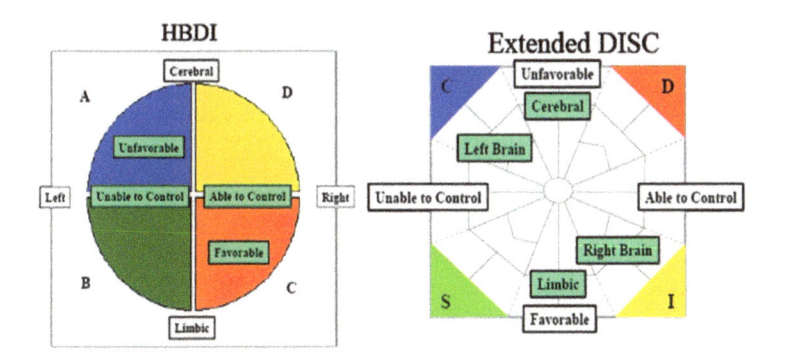

Image 29, HBDI and Extended DISC
This image created by the author: Dr. Dennis Wilson, PhD

7

A cautionary note: it is evident from this research that it is difficult to infer personality type or thinking style from a behaviour profile, and it is difficult to infer behaviour from a personality-type or thinking-preference tool. If a proper view of a person's behaviour style is sought, then a behavioural-assessment psychometric instrument should be used. If a proper view of an individual's thinking preferences is sought, then a thinking assessment tool should be used. If a proper view of an individual's personality is sought, then a personality-assessment tool should be used. Good tools will have been validated for the purpose specified.

Attitudes

Attitudes are another defining aspect of an individual. Each individual has their own complement of attitudes. Attitudes are often expressed in a person's personality, thinking, and behaviour. There is no comprehensive list of attitudes, and what does and does not qualify as an attitude is not absolutely defined. However, as a starting point, Merriam-Webster defines an attitude as a mental position with regard to a fact or state; a feeling or emotion toward a fact or state (http://www.merriam-webster.com/dictionary/attitude). From a psychological perspective, an attitude is defined as "an expression of favour or disfavour toward a person, place, thing, or event" (https://en.wikipedia.org/wiki/Attitude_(psycholog)).

A very interesting aspect regarding attitudes is that, previously, they were thought to be developed as direct responses to the environment; however, current research shows that some attitudes have a significant genetic component. A paper by Olson et al., concluded that "attitudes are learned" (Olson, Vernon, Harris, & Jang, 2001, p. 859) further reported that the environment is the largest component affecting the development of attitudes. However, it was also reported that as much as 35% of attitude variability is attributable to genetics, and that twenty-six of the thirty attitudes studied showed a genetic component. In addition, the research identified a direct correspondence between how strongly an attitude is held and the portion of the genetic component attributed to it.

Current thinking in business places considerable focus on attitudes, and Gordon Allport is reported to have referred to the theory of attitudes as "the most distinctive and indispensable concept in contemporary social psychology." (https://en.wikipedia.org/wiki/Attitude_(psychology))

Attitudes are thought to have considerable influence on behaviour and job performance.

Talents

There was a recent article in *IT World* titled "10 IT Workplace Predictions for 2016." In a demonstration of its point of view around the significance businesses are placing on talent, the article declared:

> "2016 is the year of talent—how to find it, retain it, engage it, and motivate it are at the top of organizations' to-do lists. Here, workforce management experts share their predictions for the coming year." (FLORENTINE, 2016) (http://resources.idgenterprise.com/original/AST-0163215_workplace_transform_-_citrix_v3.pdf)

Dictionary.com defines talent as "a special ability that allows someone to do something well." In the book, *First, Break All the Rules: What the World's Greatest Managers Do Differently* (Buckingham & Coffman, 1999), the authors claim a talent is "a recurring pattern of thought, feeling, or behaviour that can be productively applied" (Buckingham & Coffman, 1999, p. 71). It is important to keep in mind that Buckingham and Coffman have a very specific focus on business, and in the business environment, not all talents are important. Only the correct, role-specific talents result in excellence (Buckingham & Coffman, 1999, p. 73). Additionally, Buckingham and Coffman claim that talents cannot be taught; they have to be selected. They refer to talents as "beautiful, frictionless, traffic-free, four-lane highways" of the mind where the neural connections run smooth and strong (Buckingham & Coffman, 1999, p. 81).

Keeping in mind that there is no definitive, comprehensive list of talents, and that only role-specific talents are important in business, Buckingham and Coffman provided the following list of talents, which may be helpful in understanding their position:

Striving Talents

Achiever: A drive that is internal, constant, and self-imposed.

Kinesthetic: A need to expend physical energy.

Stamina: Capacity for physical endurance.

Competition: A need to gauge your success comparatively.

Desire: A need to claim significance through independence, excellence, risk, and recognition.

Competence: A need for expertise or mastery.

Belief: A need to orient your life around certain prevailing values.

Mission: A drive to put your beliefs into action.

Service: A drive to be of service to others.

Ethics: A clear understanding of right and wrong that guides your actions.

Vision: A drive to paint value-based word pictures about the future.

Thinking Talents

Focus: An ability to set goals and to use them every day to guide actions.

Discipline: A need to impose structure onto life and work.

Arranger: An ability to orchestrate.

Work Orientation: A need to mentally rehearse and review.

Gestalt: A need to see order and accuracy.

Responsibility: A need to assume personal accountability for your work.

Concept: An ability to develop a framework by which to make sense of things.

Performance Orientation: A need to be objective and to measure performance.

Strategic Thinking: An ability to play out alternative scenarios in the future.

Business Thinking: The financial application of the strategic thinking talent.

Problem Solving: An ability to think things through with incomplete data.

Formulation: An ability to find coherent patterns within incoherent data sets.

Numerical: An affinity for numbers.

Creativity: An ability to break existing configurations in favor of more effective/ appealing ones.

Relating Talents

Woo: A need to gain the approval of others.

Empathy: An ability to identify the feelings and perspectives of others.

Relator: A need to build bonds that last.

Multi-relator: An ability to build an extensive network of acquaintances.

Interpersonal: An ability to purposely capitalize upon relationships. **Individualized Perception**: An awareness of and attentiveness to individual differences.

Developer: A need to invest in others and to derive satisfaction in so doing.

Stimulator: An ability to create enthusiasm and drama.

Team: A need to build feelings of mutual support.

Positivity: A need to look on the bright side.

Persuasion: An ability to persuade others logically.

Command: An ability to take charge.

Activator: An impatience to move others to action.

Courage: An ability to use emotion to overcome resistance.

(Buckingham & Coffman, 1999, Appendix C)

With regards to the field of talent management, "talent" appears to get redefined as "competencies," and in contradiction to the definition provided by Buckingham and Coffman, competencies may include experience along with those aspects of an individual's behaviour that are learned, taught, or trained. The challenge will be to see if the relaxed/altered concept of talent referred to as "competencies" will yield the better performance results, or whether closely adhering to Buckingham and Coffman's perspective will yield the better performance results.

Combining Assessment Instruments

There are several different constructs that may be used to describe an individual. We can talk about the individual in terms of their personalities, intelligence, thinking, behaviour, attitudes, and aptitudes. For each of these constructs, there are psychological or psychometric instruments for assessing it and describing the individual. There has been research that shows links between personality and thinking, and research that shows links between personality, thinking, and behaviour. It does not appear as though there has been definitive research to show a relationship between intelligence and personality.

With respect to personality, thinking, and behaviour, there have been some cross-tool studies and valid relationships have been found among the various tools. Cross-validation is quite important and implies that there may also be a theoretical connection between the different tool models. If a tool (assessment instrument) is validated by another tool in the cross-validation, it suggests that the theoretical concepts behind the tools are linked in some way and therefore can be considered more robust, especially if the theoretical concepts are explained or predicted by the cross-tool validation.

In the same way, researchers, practitioners, and businesses have found that greater insight into the person and/or group can be achieved through the use of two or more psychometric instruments.

Huefner et al. studied the results of combining assessment information from the Entrepreneurial Quotient (EQ) (EQ as defined for this study), the Entrepreneurial Attitude Orientation (EAO), the Myers-Briggs Type Indicator (MBTI), and the Herrmann Brain Dominance Instrument (HBDI). The objective of the research was to determine if prediction and understanding of entrepreneurship might be enhanced by using several different types of scales. The results of the study indicated that the EQ produced the best results because of its exceptionally low misclassification of owner-managers and non-entrepreneurs as entrepreneurs. The best combination of scales was found to be the EQ, EAO, and MBTI. This produced a higher correct hit rate for entrepreneurs (62.8%). So if the goal was to minimize the number of people selected as potential entrepreneurs and eliminate those that would be better left to be owner-managers and non-entrepreneurs, then the EQ should be the instrument of choice. If the objective was to maximize the number of people selected who would have the best chance of success as entrepreneurs, then the tools of choice (based on the results of this research) would be the EQ, EAO, and MBTI in combination. (Huefner, Hunt, & Robinson, 1996)

Practical Application of Psychometric Assessments

As is often indicated in this book, psychometric assessments are commonly used in research. In addition, it is generally accepted by many, but certainly not by all, that there are many benefits to psychometric assessments. It has been generally found that psychometric assessments may be helpful in:

- Gaining an understanding of the individual.

- Gaining an understanding of group dynamics.

- Recruitment.

- Succession planning.

- Developing greater self-awareness.

- Developing greater self-esteem.

- Improving communication.

- Developing leaders.

- Decision-making.

- Understanding motivations.

- Recognizing interests.
- Building teams.
- Choosing a career path.
- Reducing stress.
- Reducing conflicts.
- Improving customer relations.
- Improved selling strategies.
- Recognizing differences.

This is not a definitive or comprehensive list. The intended here is to give some indication of the benefits that may be derived from the prudent use of psychometric assessments.

Other Popular Psychometric Products Specific To Business

As discussed above, multiple psychometric instruments may be used to garner a more robust perspective on an individual or group. In fact, the practice of using multiple psychometric instruments is not uncommon. Understanding that no single instrument (personality, thinking, behaviour, motivation, attitudes, talents, etc.) may give the desired results for a specific business interest, some developers of psychometric instruments have combined the theoretical concepts of several assessment tools into a single one in order to make it more suitable to the specific business need.

There are many psychometric instruments that are specific to business and are frequently used in business to help in choosing employees, to help employers with team-building, and to help improve the organizational structure. Some of the more notable and respected tools are the Kolbe, the Winslow, the Taylor Protocols, the California Psychological Inventory, and the FIRO business tool.

Kolbe

(http://www.kolbe.com/improveYourBusiness/improve-your-business.cfm)

Kolbe's unique collection of employee assessments and WAREwithal® software are powerful diagnostic tools that help decision-makers:

- hire and keep the right people;
- maximize employee potential;
- build successful project teams.

Kolbe also offers specialized training on the Kolbe System™ for organizational leaders, management consultants, and professional coaches through the Kolbe Certification™ program. Kolbe's fundamental approach is to identify and leverage people's natural talents. The Kolbe System's™ proven solutions allow companies to build better teams, hire successfully, develop leaders, motivate and retain employees, and resolve conflicts.

The Kolbe System is backed by more than three decades of scientific research and validation and meets the standards of the American Psychological Association for validity and reliability as well as race, gender, and age neutrality.

For more information on how Kolbe solutions can take your business to the next level, e-mail them or call (800) 642-2822.

Emergenetics

(https://www.emergenetics.com/)

According to Emergenetics, the Emergenetics Profile was developed to distinctively measure how people think and behave. With this insight, you can develop personal strategies to get results. Developed through years of psychometric research, the Emergenetics Profile accurately measures three behavioural attributes (expressiveness, assertiveness, and flexibility) and four thinking attributes (analytical, structural, social, and conceptual). The attributes are represented in a clear, colour-coded report, making it memorable and applicable immediately.

The Emergenetics instrument was developed by Drs. Geil Browning and Wendell Williams to combine the core principles of effective learning, communication styles, and team interaction. The 100-item questionnaire is the product of extensive social research proven to reliably capture the major thinking and behavioural preferences people commonly use.

Emergenetics meets professional test development criteria defined by the 1999 Standards for Educational and Psychological Testing. It has been validated for both its content (e.g., r= .43 to r=.67, using independent third-party observers); and its construct (e.g., using a Big-Five universally accepted measure of personality). The Emergenetics instrument meets inter-item reliability standards (e.g., between r=.76 and r=.83, depending on the factor), and its test-retest reliability is given as: r= .68 and r=.77 based on 415 people over ten years.

The authors of the Emergentic instrument submit that, while no psychometric tool can truly capture the complexity and richness of the human mind-brain-body, the Emergenetics model is grounded firmly in professional psychological survey design and provides a practical and effective tool for successful individual and team communication within virtually any situation.

Winslow

(http://winslowresearch.com/)
A human behaviour assessment system

Founded in 1968, Winslow Research Institute applies forty-five years of research and development to the creation of powerful human behaviour assessment programs. The Winslow Assessment Systems (assessment profiles, interpretative reports, and related components) were authored and validated by a distinguished panel of psychologists and business executives to measure the personality and behaviour of individuals in a wide variety of applications. This is significant because, according to the Winslow development team, personality and behaviour are the most relevant predictors of success in both careers and personal lifestyles.

According to the Winslow organization, assessment of personality traits provides more insight into individuals than behavioural-style assessments, which merely categorize participants. According to Winslow, their instrument measures more traits and provides more comprehensive feedback. Winslow claims their instrument has more features than any other assessment instrument. This all translates to a much more efficient method of employee screening and individual assessment.

Exclusive assessment validity controls assure the most accurate and objective profiles available (control scales are not included in other profiles). Plain language delivers instant understanding to both participants and management. Position Success Profiles, provided at no additional fee, enable clients to compare the personality of employees and applicants to the behavioural requirements of their positions. Private end-user client websites enable clients to administer and organize all aspects of their assessment activity. A secure internet purchasing system enables clients to make purchases electronically and immediately receive profile passwords. A comprehensive internet assessment processing system facilitates the scoring of the profiles, the preparation of the interpretive reports, and other program components. The major applications for the Winslow Reports are employee development, employee screening, applicant selection, personal coaching, and personal self-improvement.

Taylor Protocols

(http://www.taylorprotocols.com/)

According to the Taylor Protocols organization, their instrument is the only instrument proven to identify top-performing candidates. The Core Value Index (CVI) reveals the unchanging nature of an individual with the most reliable assessment ever created. It characterizes and quantifies what Abraham Maslow called the unchanging innate nature of a person that inscribes where a person can make their highest and most productive contribution to the world. The Core Value Index has been proven in longitudinal studies to have 94% repeat-score reliability (other assessments typically provide a reliability between of 60% and 80%). Taylor Protocols provide a clear and useful picture of the innate unchanging nature of an individual.

The CVI is not a personality and behaviour assessment, but the only human assessment that uses strategic and tactical values and a forced-choice format in order to gain unequivocal insight into the innate nature of a person. The CVI is comprised of only positive values. No negative disclosure is required, and no context is provided. The Taylor Protocols organization promotes its instrument as the only assessment that should be used as a pre-screening tool for an employment-application process.

California Psychological Inventory (CPI)

(https://www.psychometrics.com/assessments/cpi-434/)

Built on fifty-plus years of exceptional history, validity, and reliability, the California Psychological Inventory assessments are powerful leadership development and selection tools that help individuals and leaders improve their performance. Both the CPI 260 in the CPI 434 assessments provide valuable insights that support leadership coaching, performance improvement, and selection initiatives. By describing individuals in the way others see them, the CPI assessment illustrates a range of personal and work-related characteristics, motivations, and thinking styles, as well as different ways people manage themselves and deal with others.

FIRO Business

(https://www.psychometrics.com/assessments/firo-business/)

FIRO Business provides insight into communication styles and behaviours that affect leadership performance. For more than fifty years, the Fundamental Interpersonal Relations Orientation (FIRO) approach has helped people understand their interpersonal needs and how they influence their communication styles and behaviour. Building on the history and reliability of the FIRO model, CPP has developed the FIRO business assessment to address the specific requirements of organizations. The FIRO Business Leadership Report is particularly valuable to businesses because it presents key insights for relating to direct reports, superiors, and peers; influencing and negotiating; making decisions; and setting priorities. CPP claims the report is a must-use tool for leadership development and executive coaching.

Cautionary Note:

Again, it is important to remember that this is not an exhaustive list of psychometric instruments. What's here is simply meant to convey a perspective on the range of quality psychometric instruments available to businesses and other organizations.

Psychometric Assessments and the Workplace

It is often posited whether a person's supervisor or prospective employer should have access to their psychometric assessment information. The law (somewhat dependent on the jurisdiction) generally states that no one may access a person's psychometric assessment information without the subject's permission. However, individual judgment and opinion are an acceptable and uncontrolled aspect of business. For someone to make a subjective judgment with respect to some aspect of a person's character is an acceptable and uncontrolled reality of life. In other words, instead of having a person complete some form of psychometric assessment—whether it be a personality, thinking, behaviour, or other type—a consultant may be contracted who, through the process of an interview, may develop a subjective opinion about the person's personality type. Furthermore, a consultant may form a subjective opinion on what the person's thinking preferences, behaviour style, and talents might be, and may form an opinion with respect to any other aspect of the person's psyche. Once they have, it is quite acceptable for the consultant to convey this subjective assessment to the person or organization that has contracted their services. This is entirely legal regardless of jurisdiction, and it is an accepted business practice.

So, the question becomes about what would you prefer: a subjective judgment formed by a consultant with regards to your personality, thinking, behaviour, etc., or an empirical assessment of your personality, thinking, behaviour, etc.? A person has no control over the formulation of subjective opinions, and there is no empirical measure of the quality of those opinions. If psychometric assessments are significantly curtailed, I suspect there would be greater demand for the services of those individuals capable of forming subjective opinions.

Advancing the Topic

Psychology is not a topic that is typically part of the high school curriculum. "The reality is that the first exposure most students have to psychology is when they take Psych 101 during their first year of college" (http://psychology.about.com/od/education/f/psychology-classes-for-high-school-students.htm, March 26, 2016). A search for business programs that provide course work in human psychology, or even psychology, did not produce any results. To clarify, there were courses in human-resources management in many business programs, but those courses tended to approach the subject matter from an administrative and legal perspective, and not from the perspective of managing human capital. They did not have specific coursework on the psychological aspects of humans as they pertain to the workspace.

In some business programs, students may be encouraged to enroll in an introductory psychology program, but these programs tend to be very broad and general. They have relatively little content that is focused specifically on the work-related aspects of human psychology, and they tend to be more tailored to those students that are likely to pursue further studies in psychology itself.

There is definitely a need to support those individuals who have an interest in acquiring and/or improving their knowledge of human psychology as it applies to the workspace. To this end, as has already been mentioned, look to Wikipedia and a number of topic-specific websites supported by academic institutions and private organizations. In addition, LinkedIn is also an incredible resource for some of the most pressing questions and best thought leadership. There are hundreds if not thousands of groups on LinkedIn that deal with the subject matter from a neurological, human-resource, human-capital, organizational-psychology, human-psychology, and pure-psychology perspective.

Some business courses with a human-psychology perspective may focus on the marketing-related aspects of human psychology, but the field of understanding relevant to business is much larger than simply marketing, so this focus also ends up being limited.

LinkedIn is a substantial source of ongoing support. The following excerpts from that site provide a very limited view of the exposure to the subject area and, as indicated above, offer access to both the most advanced knowledge and some of the best thought leadership.

American Society for Biochemistry and Molecular Biology

The American Society for Biochemistry and Molecular Biology (ASBMB) is a nonprofit scientific and educational organization with over 12,000 members.

Founded in 1906, the society is based in Bethesda, Maryland, on the campus of the Federation of American Societies for Experimental Biology. The society's purpose is to advance the science of biochemistry and molecular biology through the publication of scientific and educational journals (including the *Journal of Biological Chemistry, Molecular & Cellular Proteomics* and the *Journal of Lipid Research*), the organization of scientific meetings, advocacy for funding of basic research and education, support of science education at all levels, and the promotion of the diversity of individuals entering the scientific workforce.

Australian Human Resources Institute

This group promotes meaningful discussions on all things HR, with two main rules:

1. The only posts allowed are discussions that can be commented on without needing to follow a link.

2. If your post sparks, questions, or contrary opinions you should respond.

The AHRI is Australia's only association for human resources. It leads the direction and fosters the growth of the profession through actively setting standards and building capabilities.

This group is managed and moderated by AHRI staff. Other groups displaying the AHRI networks logo are managed by AHRI volunteer members and AHRI does not monitor those sites. If you wish to contact AHRI directly, call +61 (0)3 9918 9200 during business hours.

Human Resources Professionals (HR Professionals)

The HR Professionals group was established to promote networking and idea and practice sharing, and to better the oversight of human resources in companies.

Human Resources (HR) & Talent Management Executive

HR and Talent Management Executives claims to be the number-one talent-management group on LinkedIn.

The group includes over 400,000 industry professionals from around the world. This is a very active group and all submissions are moderated, which means you'll save time for not having to sort through thousands of off-topic posts and spam to find quality content.

Human Capital Institute (HCI)

The Human Capital Institute is a global association for strategic talent management. It is an executive association with 195,000 members. Growing at more than 2,000 members a month, its members are senior HR and line executives from 92% of the Fortune 1000, thousands of mid-size companies, and scores of government agencies in over 170 countries.

Its members interact with the organization, each other, and its underwriters in one of four integrated channels:

- Online: HCI's destination site contains the world's premium archive of on-demand, mobile-enabled information on strategic talent management and is powered by the latest tools in web-based collaboration and content.

- Research: It conducts major studies every year in talent strategy, acquisition, development, and leadership, and distributes that content to thousands of executives and practitioners around the world.

- Education: It has educated thousands of individuals from some of the world's best companies, and it offers the only certification programs in human capital strategy and workforce planning available today.

- Events: Unique in the market, HCI events are executively strategic, senior in audience, and education-based, providing a forum for members to come together to shape debate and move the practice of human capital management forward.

Human Capital Management Excellence

This is a group for those interested in thought leadership, research, and data across the human-capital-management spectrum, including areas such as learning and development, talent management, leadership development, talent acquisition, human resources, and workforce management.

Psychology in Human Resources (Organizational Psychology)

The focus is on industry and organizational psychology, psychology in human resources and business psychology at work.

This group has been formulated to network and share experiences and accepts industry professionals, students, and individuals interested in business psychology.

The Business Psychology at Work group provides a forum for sharing thoughts and obtaining valuable feedback from business psychology professionals. It is a great networking opportunity that offers useful tips on improving a company's true potential.

The Human Element—Organizational Behaviour

Established to promote the psychology behind successful businesses and organizations, the group promotes the development and understanding of the human element as an area of business that's often overlooked. The more we understand our people—really know them, and how they think, act, learn, make decisions, and change under stress—the more significant a difference we can make to the success of both the business and the individual.

This group is designed to exchange and share ideas to help business professionals promote the development of their teams and individuals by understanding the latest thinking in human and organizational psychology.

The forgoing was a very abbreviated list of the knowledge and expertise available on LinkedIn.

In Review

It has been argued that people are the most valuable asset of any corporation. This book has been written in the interest of preserving and enhancing the value of that asset. It is intended to offer the reader an understanding of the differences in people and a relatively small portion of the available information as a basis from which they might pursue a more in-depth study of human psychology on their own initiative, especially from a business perspective.

This book has presented the concept that genetics provide the initial prescription for human development, and that the genetic prescription is modified by environmental experiences in the developmental years of early childhood. Some say that basic personality is established by the age of five (http://developingchild.harvard.edu/resources/inbrief-science-of-ecd/, 14-Mar-16); others say basic personality is established by the age of seven, and still others assert that personality is basically stable by the age of ten. What is fairly certain is that basic personality is well established before a person enters their teenage years and that it tends to remain consistent through a person's life.

This text has also stated that there is new technology that provides very clear images of the brain. It enables researchers to observe brain function, and it helps identify the functional pathways. The book provides a high-level and general discussion of the nervous system and the biological mechanism at work there. The discussion presents the concept of differential performance resulting from performance differences in the biological mechanism. In the text it is suggested that biology is at the root of these differences and the consistency ascribed to personality.

The text also presents the proposition that, in some cases, new research at the physiological level is supportive of some psychological theories, and that some of those theories have been around for many decades. It promotes the view that there are well-founded psychological theories dealing with the nature and performance of individuals that are supported by research in both physiology and psychology. Some of the more robust among them have been incorporated into the design of many psychometric instruments. Many of the more popular psychometric instruments have respectable validity and reliability measures, indicating that they provide information that is consistent and representative of the psychological construct each purports to represent. It has also been indicated that psychometric instruments may be combined in order to provide a more comprehensive description of the individual.

In addition, this text has provided a concise overview of some of the more popular psychometric instruments currently in use by businesses. It is hoped that this will be of some help to the reader who may be looking to add them to the human-capital-management practices within their organization.

Image 30, Clydesdales   Image 31, Racehorse

The Right Horse for the Job

Consider the two pictures above. Image 30 is a picture of a couple of Clydesdale horses and Image 31 is a picture of a couple of thoroughbred horses. The Clydesdale is definitely a workhorse and the thoroughbred is definitely a racehorse. It is highly unlikely that a Clydesdale would win a race against a thoroughbred, and it is highly unlikely that you would get as much heavy work done using a thoroughbred, as compared to a Clydesdale. The takeaway from this—figuratively speaking—is that you need to get the right horse for the job. With regards to people, and from the perspective of Buckingham and Coffman, a business needs to employ the people with the right talents for specific roles, and then to develop those people so that they can perform at their very best. The idea is to see a person for who they really are, and to reach to understand what makes them so.

Index

Brain Structure
  amygdala, 32
  Brain Stem, 31
  Brodmann areas, 36
  Cerebellum, 32
  Cerebral Cortex, 35
  Cerebrum, 34
  Corpus Callosum, 35
  Cortex, 35
  hippocampus, 33
  hypothalamus, 33
  Limbic System, 32
  thalamus, 34

Decision Making
  Inappropriate attachments, 53
  Inappropriate Self-interest, 52
  Misleading experiences, 50
  Misleading Pre-judgments, 51

Emotional Intelligence
  Empathy, 81
  Facilitating thought, 82
  Managing emotions, 80, 83
  Mixed Model, 81
  Motivation, 81
  Perceiving emotions, 80, 82
  Self-awareness, 81
  Self-regulation, 81
  Social skill, 81
  Trait Model, 81
  Understanding emotions, 80, 83
  Using emotions, 80

Endorphins, 19
  Extroverts, 64

Hand Exercise, 41

Intelligence
  Crystallized intelligence, 74
  Fluid intelligence, 74

Introverts, 63

Neuronal Pathways, 25
  Auditory System, 26
  Gustatory System, 28
  Olfactory System, 27
  Visual System, 25

Neurons, 7

Action on other neurons, 16
  Cholinergic neurons, 18

Classification by Neurotransmitter ,18
Dopaminergic neurons ,18
Glutamatergic neurons ,18
Life of a Neuron ,7
Neural coding ,24
Number of Neurons in the brain ,20
Serotonergic neurons ,19

Neurons and Drugs ,21
Caffeine ,22
Nicotine ,21
Opiates (Heroin) ,21

Runners High ,20

Synapse ,11
Action on other neurons ,16
All-or-none principle ,15
Chemical Synapse ,12
Electrical Synapse ,13
Synapse and Memory ,14

Talents
Relating Talents ,113
Striving Talents ,112
Thinking Talents ,112

The Whole Brain Model ,100

What great managers know ,65